Harvard Business Review

ON

EMERGING MARKETS

THE HARVARD BUSINESS REVIEW PAPERBACK SERIES

The series is designed to bring today's managers and professionals the fundamental information they need to stay competitive in a fast-moving world. From the preeminent thinkers whose work has defined an entire field to the rising stars who will redefine the way we think about business, here are the leading minds and landmark ideas that have established the *Harvard Business Review* as required reading for ambitious businesspeople in organizations around the globe.

Other books in the series:

Other books in the series (continued):

Harvard Business Review on Decision Making
Harvard Business Review on Developing Leaders
Harvard Business Review on Doing Business in China
Harvard Business Review on Effective Communication
Harvard Business Review on Entrepreneurship
Harvard Business Review on Finding and Keeping the Best People
Harvard Business Review on Green Business Strategy
Harvard Business Review on the High-Performance Organization
Harvard Business Review on Innovation
Harvard Business Review on the Innovative Enterprise
Harvard Business Review on Knowledge Management
Harvard Business Review on Leadership
Harvard Business Review on Leadership at the Top
Harvard Business Review on Leadership in a Changed World
Harvard Business Review on Leading in Turbulent Times
Harvard Business Review on Leading Through Change
Harvard Business Review on Making Smarter Decisions
Harvard Business Review on Managing Diversity
Harvard Business Review on Managing Health Care
Harvard Business Review on Managing High-Tech Industries
Harvard Business Review on Managing People
Harvard Business Review on Managing Projects
Harvard Business Review on Managing Uncertainty
Harvard Business Review on Managing the Value Chain
Harvard Business Review on Managing Your Career
Harvard Business Review on Managing Yourself
Harvard Business Review on Marketing
Harvard Business Review on Measuring Corporate Performance
Harvard Business Review on Mergers and Acquisitions

Harvard Business Review

ON

EMERGING MARKETS

A HARVARD BUSINESS REVIEW PAPERBACK

The *Harvard Business Review* articles in this collection are available as
individual reprints. Discounts apply to quantity purchases. For information and ordering, please contact Customer Service, Harvard Business
School Publishing, Boston, MA 02163. Telephone: (617) 783-7500 or
(800) 988-0886, 8 A.M. to 6 P.M. Eastern Time, Monday through Friday.
Fax: (617) 783-7555, 24 hours a day. E-mail: custserv@hbsp.harvard.edu.

Library of Congress Cataloging-in-Publication Data
Harvard business review on emerging markets.
        p.   cm. — (A Harvard business review paperback)
    Includes index.
    ISBN-978-1-4221-2649-3
    1. Developing countries—Commerce.   2. International business
enterprises—Developing countries.   I. Harvard business review.
HF1413.H353   2008
658.8′4091724—dc22   2008010439

Contents

Harvard Business Review

ON

EMERGING MARKETS

Local Memoirs of a Global Manager

GURCHARAN DAS

Executive Summary

"THINK GLOBAL, ACT LOCAL" goes the saying. But Gurcharan Das, who helped build Vicks Vaporub into one of Procter & Gamble's most successful Indian brands, believes that "think local" is just as important. The key to global success, he argues, is local passion.

After a childhood in India and high school and college in the United States, Das went home to work for Vicks and help with the building of a young nation. He learned invaluable lessons about local focus and the central importance of the customer. Ironically, he points out, all a company's income is made outside the organization at the point of sale, yet employees spend all their time inside the organization (usually fighting over turf). When Das himself became CEO, he made a rule that all employees in all departments had to go out each year and meet 20 consumers and 20 retailers or wholesalers in order to qualify for their annual raises.

Always, he cultivated local roots, institutions, and traditions. The company adapted native distribution networks rather than build its own, it created special sizes and prices for the Indian poor, it put together a marketing campaign based on the Indian monsoon, and eventually it used ancient Sanskrit texts to help it develop additional all-natural, herbal products.

The most successful global brands, Das argues, are those that make best use of the rich experience their geographical diversity gives them. Business truths are invariably local in origin; but they are often expressions of fundamental human needs that are the same world-wide. Flexible, open-minded managers can take local insights and make them global. In the end, local and global thinking are both aspects of the kind of commitment that is essential to business success—and to personal happiness.

THERE WAS A TIME when I used to believe with Diogenes the Cynic that "I am a citizen of the world," and I used to strut about feeling that a "blade of grass is always a blade of grass, whether in one country or another." Now I feel that each blade of grass has its spot on earth from where it draws its life, its strength; and so is man rooted to the land from where he draws his faith, together with his life.

In India, I was privileged to help build one of the largest businesses in the world for Vicks Vaporub, a hundred-year-old brand sold in 147 countries and now owned by Procter & Gamble. In the process, I learned a number of difficult and valuable lessons about business and about myself. The most important lesson was this: to learn to tap into the roots of diversity in a world where global standardization plays an increasingly useful role.

The fact is that truths in this world are unique, individual, and highly parochial. They say all politics is local. So is all business. But this doesn't keep either from being global. In committing to our work we commit to a here and now, to a particular place and time; but what we learn from acting locally is often universal in nature.

This is how globalization takes place. Globalization does not mean imposing homogeneous solutions in a pluralistic world. It means having a global vision and strategy, but it also means cultivating roots and individual identities. It means nourishing local insights, but it also means reemploying communicable ideas in new geographies around the world.

The more human beings belong to their own time and place, the more they belong to *all* times and places. Today's best global managers know this truth. They nourish each "blade of grass."

Managerial basics are the same everywhere, in the West and in the Third World. There is a popular misconception among managers that you need merely to push a powerful brand name with a standard product, package, and advertising in order to conquer global markets, but actually the key to success is a tremendous amount of local passion for the brand and a feeling of local pride and ownership.

I learned these lessons as a manager of international brands in the Third World and as a native of India struggling against the temptation to stay behind in the West.

On Going Home

I was four years old when India became free. Before they left, the British divided us into two countries, India and Pakistan, and on a monsoon day in August 1947 I suddenly became a refugee. I had to flee east for my life because I was a Hindu in predominantly Muslim West Punjab. I survived, but a million others did not, and another 12 million were rendered homeless in one of the great tragedies of our times.

I grew up in a middle-class home in East Punjab as the eldest son of a civil engineer who built canals and dams for the government. Our family budget was always tight: after paying for milk and school fees, there was little left to run the house. My mother told us heroic stories from the *Mahabharata* and encouraged in us the virtues of honesty, thrift, and responsibility to country.

I grew up in the innocence of the Nehru age when we still had strong ideals. We believed in secularism, democracy, socialism, and the U.N.; and we were filled with the excitement of building a nation.

I came to the United States at the age of 12, when the Indian government sent my father to Washington, D.C. on temporary assignment. When my family returned to India a few years later, I won a scholarship to Harvard College and spent four happy years on the banks of the Charles River. My tutor taught me that the sons of Harvard had an obligation to serve, and I knew that I must one day use my education to serve India.

In 1964, in the towering confidence of my 21 years, I returned home. Some of my friends thought I had made a mistake. They said I should have gone on to graduate school and worked for a few years in the West. In fact, I missed the West in the beginning and told myself that I would go back before long; but I soon became absorbed in my new job with Richardson-Vicks in Bombay, and like the man who came to dinner, I stayed on.

From a trainee, I rose to become CEO of the company's Indian subsidiary, with interim assignments at Vicks headquarters in New York and in the Mexican subsidiary. When I became CEO, the Indian company was almost bankrupt, but with the help of a marvelous all-Indian organization, I turned it around in the early 1980s and made it one of the most profitable companies on the Bombay Stock Exchange. In 1985 we were acquired by Procter & Gamble, and so began another exciting chapter in my life. We successfully incorporated the company into P&G without losing a single employee, and we put ourselves on an aggressive growth path, with an entry first into sanitary napkins and then into one of the largest detergent markets in the world.

At three stages in my life, I was tempted to settle in the West. Each time I could have chosen to lead the cosmopolitan life of an expatriate. Each time I chose to return home. The first after college; the second when I was based in the New York office of Vicks, where I met my Nepali wife with her coveted Green Card (which we allowed to lapse); the third when I was in Mexico running our nutritional foods business, when once again I came home to earn a fraction of what I would have earned abroad.

Apart from a lurking wish to appear considerable in the eyes of those I grew up with, I ask myself why I keep returning to India. I have thrice opted for what appeared to be the less rational course in terms of career and money. The only remotely satisfying answer I have found comes from an enigmatic uncle of mine who once said, "You've come back, dear boy, because as a child you listened to the music of your mother's voice. They all say, 'I'll be back in a few years,' but the few years become many, until it is too late and you are lost in a lonely and homeless crowd."

Yet I think of myself as a global manager within the P&G world. I believe my curious life script has helped to create a mind-set that combines the particular with the universal, a mind-set rooted in the local and yet open and nonparochial, a mind-set I find useful in the global management of P&G brands.

On One-Pointed Success

I first arrived on the island of Bombay on a monsoon day after eight years of high school and college in America. That night, 15-foot waves shattered thunderously against the rocks below my window as the rain advanced from the Arabian sea like the disciplined forward phalanx of an army.

The next morning I reported for duty at Richardson-Vicks' Indian headquarters, which turned out to be a rented hole-in-the-wall with a dozen employees. This was a change after the company's swank New York offices in midtown Manhattan, where I had been interviewed. That evening my cousin invited me for dinner. He worked in a big British company with many factories, thousands of employees, and plush multistoried marble offices. I felt ashamed to talk about my job.

"How many factories do you have?" he wanted to know.

"None," I said.

"How many salesmen do you have?" he asked.

"None," I said.

"How many employees?"

"Twelve."

"How big are your offices?"

"A little smaller than your house."

Years later I realized that what embarrassed me that night turned out to be our strength. All twelve of our employees were focused on building our brands without the distraction of factories, sales forces, industrial relations, finance and other staff departments. Our products were made under contract by Boots, an English drug company; they were distributed under contract by an outside distribution house with 100 salesmen spread around the country; our external auditors had arranged for someone to do our accounting; and our lawyers took care of our government work. We were lean, nimble, focused, and very profitable.

All my cousin's talk that night revolved around office politics, and all his advice was about how to get around the office bureaucracy. It was not clear to me how his company made decisions. But he was a smart man, and I sensed that with all his pride in working for a giant organization, he had little respect for its bureaucratic style.

If marketing a consumer product is what gives a company its competitive advantage, then it seems to me it should spend all its time building marketing and product muscle and employ outside suppliers to do everything else. It should spin off as many services as someone else is willing to take on and leave everyone inside the company focused on one thing—creating, retaining, and satisfying consumers.

There is a concept in Yoga called one-pointedness (from the Sanskrit *Ekagrata*). All twelve of us were one-pointedly focused on making Vicks a household name in India, as if we were 12 brand managers. I now teach our younger managers the value of a one-pointed focus on consumer satisfaction, which P&G measures every six months for all of its major brands.

Concentrating on one's core competence thus was one of the first lessons I learned. I learned it because I was face-to-face with the consumer, focused on the particular. Somehow I feel it would have taken me longer to learn this lesson in a glass tower in Manhattan.

As so often in life, however, by the time I could apply the lesson I had learned, we had a thousand people, with factories, sales forces, and many departments that were having a lot of fun fighting over turf. I believe that tomorrow's big companies may well consist of hundreds of small decentralized units, each with a sharp focus on its particular customers and markets.

On the Kettle That Wrote My Paycheck

For months I believed that my salary came from the payroll clerk, so I was especially nice to her. (She was also the boss's secretary.) Then one day I discovered the most important truth of my career—I realized who really paid my salary.

Soon after I joined the company, my boss handed me a bag and a train ticket and sent me "up-country." A man of the old school, he believed that you learned marketing only in the bazaar, so I spent 10 of my first 15 months on the road and saw lots of up-country bazaars.

On the road, I typically would meet our trade customers in the mornings and consumers in the evenings. In the afternoons everyone slept. One evening I knocked on the door of a middle-class home in Surat, a busy trading town 200 miles north of Bombay. The lady of the house reluctantly let me in. I asked her, "What do you use for your family's coughs and colds?" Her eyes lit up, her face became animated. She told me that she had discovered the most wonderful solution. She went into the kitchen and brought back a jar of Vicks Vaporub and a kettle. She then showed me how she poured a spoon of Vaporub into the boiling kettle and inhaled the medicated vapors from the spout.

"If you don't believe me, try it for yourself," she said. "Here, let me boil some water for you."

Before I could reply she had disappeared into the kitchen. Instead of drinking tea that evening we inhaled Vicks Vaporub. As I walked back to my hotel, I felt intoxicated: I had discovered it was she who paid my salary. My job also became clear to me: I must reciprocate her compliment by striving relentlessly to satisfy her needs.

The irony is that all the money a company makes is made *outside* the company (at the point of sale), yet the employees spend their time *inside* the company, usually arguing over turf. Unfortunately, we don't see customers around us when we show up for work in the mornings.

When I became the CEO of the company I made a rule that every employee in every department had to go out every year and meet 20 consumers and 20 retailers or wholesalers in order to qualify for their annual raise. This not only helps to remind us who pays our salaries, we also get a payoff in good ideas to improve our products and services.

The idea of being close to the customer may be obvious in the commercial societies of the West, but it was not so obvious 20 years ago in the protected, bureaucratic Indian environment. As to the lady in Surat, we quickly put her ideas into our advertising. She was the first consumer to show me a global insight in my own backyard.

Of Chairs, Armchairs, and Monsoons

Two years after I joined, I was promoted. I was given Vicks Vaporub to manage, which made me the first brand manager in the company. I noticed we were building volume strongly in the South but having trouble in the North. I asked myself whether I should try to fix the North or capitalize on the momentum in the South. I chose the latter, and it was the right choice. We later discovered that North Indians don't like to rub things on their bodies, yet the more important lesson was that it is usually better to build on your strength than to try and correct a weakness. Listen to and respect the market. Resist the temptation to impose your will on it.

We were doing well in the South partially because South Indians were accustomed to rubbing on balms for headaches, colds, bodyaches, insect bites, and a host of other minor maladies. We had a big and successful balm competitor, Amrutanjan, who offered relief for all these symptoms. My first impulse was to try to expand the use of Vaporub to other symptoms in order to compete in this larger balm market.

My boss quickly and wisely put a stop to that. In an uncharacteristically loud voice, he explained that Vaporub's unique function was to relieve colds.

"Each object has a function," he said. "A chair's function is to seat a person. A desk is to write on. You don't want to use a chair for writing and a desk for sitting. You never want to mix up functions."

A great part of Vaporub's success in India has been its clear and sharp position in the consumer's mind. It is cold relief in a jar, which a mother rubs tenderly on her child's chest at bedtime. As I thought more about balms, I realized that they were quite the opposite. Adults rub balms on themselves for headaches during the day.

Vaporub was succeeding precisely because it was not a balm; it was a rub for colds.

Every brand manager since has had to learn that same lesson. It is of the utmost importance to know who you are and not be led astray by others. Tap into your roots when you are unsure. You cannot be all things to all people.

This did not prevent us from building a successful business with adults, but as my boss used to say, "Adult colds, that is an armchair. But it is still a chair and not a desk."

When I took over the brand we were spending most of our advertising rupees in the winter, a strategy that worked in North America and other countries. However, my monthly volume data stubbornly suggested that we were shipping a lot of Vaporub between July and September, the hot monsoon season. "People must be catching lots of colds in the monsoon," I told my boss, and I got his agreement to bring forward a good chunk of our media to the warm monsoon months. Sure enough, we were rewarded with an immediate gain in sales.

I followed this up by getting our agency to make a cinema commercial (we had no television at that time) showing a child playing in the rain and catching cold. We coined a new ailment, "wet monsoon colds," and soon the summer monsoon season became as important as the winter in terms of sales.

Another factor in our success was the introduction of a small 5-gram tin, which still costs 10 cents and accounts for 40% of our volume. At first it was not successful, so we had to price it so that it was cheaper to buy four 5-gram tins than a 19-gram jar. The trade thought we were crazy. They said henceforth no one would buy the profitable jar; they would trade down to the tin. But that didn't happen. Why? Because we had positioned the tin for the working

class. We were right in believing that middle class consumers would stay loyal to the middle-class size.

Moves like these made us hugely successful and
placed us first in the Indian market share by far. But
instead of celebrating, my boss seemed depressed. He
called me into his office, and he asked me how much the
market was growing.

"Seven percent," I said.

"Is that good?"

"No," I replied. "But *we* are growing 20%, and that's
why we're now number one in India."

"I don't give a damn that we are number one in a
small pond. That pond has to become a lake, and then an
ocean. We have to grow the market. Only then will we
become number one in the world."

Thus I acquired another important mind-set: when
you are number one, you must not grow complacent.
Your job is to grow the market. You always must bench-
mark yourself against the best in the world, not just
against the local competition. In the Third World this is
an especially valuable idea, because markets there are so
much less competitive.

Being receptive to regional variations, tapping the
opportunity that the monsoon offered, introducing a size
for the rural and urban poor, and learning to resist com-
placency and grow the market—all are variations on the
theme of local thinking, of tapping into the roots of pluralism and diversity.

On Not Reinventing the Wheel

We could not have succeeded in building the Vicks business in India without the support of the native traders
who took our products deep into the hinterland, to every

nook and corner of a very large country. Many times we faced the temptation to set up an alternative Western-style distribution network. Fortunately, we never gave in to it. Instead, we chose each time to continue relying on the native system.

Following the practice of British companies in India, we appointed the largest wholesaler in each major town to become our exclusive stock point and direct customer. We called this wholesaler our stockist. Once a month our salesman visited the stockist, and together they went from shop to shop redistributing our products to the retailers and wholesalers of the town. The largest stockist in each state also became our Carrying-and-Forwarding Agent (in other words, our depot) for reshipping our goods to stockists in smaller towns. Over time, our stockists expanded their functions. They now work exclusively on P&G business under the supervision of our salesmen; they hire local salesmen who provide interim coverage of the market between the visits of our salesmen; they run vans to cover satellite villages and help us penetrate the interior; they conduct local promotions and advertising campaigns; and they are P&G's ambassadors and lifeline in the local community. The stockists perform all these services for a 5% commission, and our receivables are down to six days outstanding.

In our own backyard, we found and adopted an efficient low-cost distribution system perfected by Indian traders over hundreds of years. Thank God we chose to build on it rather than reinvent the wheel.

On Taking Ancient Medicine

We learned our most important lesson about diversity and tapping into roots shortly after I became head of the company in the early 1980s. We found ourselves against a wall. The chemists and pharmacists had united nation-wide and decided to target our company and boycott our products in their fight for higher margins from the entire industry. At the same time, productivity at our plant was falling, while wages kept rising. As a result, our prof-itability had plummeted to 2% of sales.

Beset by a hostile environment, we turned inward. The answer to our problems came as a flash of insight about our roots, for we suddenly realized that Vicks Vaporub and other Vicks products were all-natural, herbal formulas. All their ingredients were found in thousand-year-old Sanskrit texts. What was more, this ancient *Ayurvedic* system of medicine enjoyed the spe-cial patronage of the government. If we could change our government registration from Western medicine to Indian medicine, we could expand our distribution to food shops, general stores, and street kiosks and thus reduce dependence on the pharmacists. By making our products more accessible, we would enhance consumer satisfaction and build competitive advantage. What was more, a new registration would also allow us to set up a new plant for Vicks in a tax-advantaged "backward area," where we could raise productivity dramatically by means of improved technology, better work practices, and lower labor costs.

I first tested the waters with our lawyers, who thought our solution to the problem quite wonderful. We then went to the government in Delhi, which was deeply impressed to discover all the elements of Vaporub's for-mula in the ancient texts. They advised us to check with the local FDA in Bombay. The regulators at the FDA couldn't find a single fault with our case and, to our sur-prise and delight, promptly gave us a new registration.

Lo and behold, all the obstacles were gone! Our sales force heroically and rapidly expanded the distribution of our products to the nondrug trade, tripling the outlets which carried Vicks to roughly 750,000 stores. Consumers were happy that they could buy our products at every street corner. At the same time we quickly built a new plant near Hyderabad, where productivity was four times what it was in our Bombay plant. Our after-tax profits rose from 2% to 12% of sales, and we became a blue chip on the Bombay Stock Exchange.

Finally, we decided to return the compliment to the Indian system of medicine. We persuaded our headquarters to let us establish an R&D Center to investigate additional all-natural, Ayurvedic therapies for coughs and colds. When I first mooted this idea, my bosses at the head office in the United States practically fell off their chairs. Slowly, however, the idea of all-natural, safe, and effective remedies for a self-limiting ailment sold around the world under the Vicks name grew on them.

We set up labs in Bombay under the leadership of a fine Indian scientist who had studied in the United States. They began by creating a computerized data bank of herbs and formulas from the ancient texts; they invented a "finger-printing" process to standardize herbal raw materials with the help of computers; and they organized clinical trials in Bombay hospitals to confirm the safety and efficacy of the new products. We now have two products being successfully sold in the Indian market—Vicks Vaposyrup, an all-natural cough liquid, and Vicks Hot-sip, a hot drink for coughs and colds. The lab today is part of P&G's global health-care research effort and has 40 scientists and technicians working with state-of-the-art equipment.

Of Local Passions and Golden Ghettos

The story of Vicks in India brings up a mistaken notion about how multinationals build global brands. The popular conception is that you start with a powerful brand name, add standardized product, packaging and advertising, push a button, and bingo—you are on the way to capturing global markets. Marlboro, Coke, Sony Walkman, and Levis are cited as examples of this strategy.

But if it's all so easy, why have so many powerful brands floundered? Without going into the standardization vs. adaptation debate, the Vicks story demonstrates at least one key ingredient for global market success: *the importance of local passion.* If local managers believe a product is theirs, then local consumers will believe it too. Indeed, a survey of Indian consumers a few years ago showed that 70% believed Vicks was an Indian brand.

What is the universal idea behind Vicks Vaporub's success in India? What is it that made it sell? Was it "rubbing it on the child with tender, loving care?" Could that idea be revived in the United States? Some people argue that the United States has become such a rushed society that mothers no longer have time to use a bedtime rub on their children when they've got a cold. Others feel that Vaporub could make its marketing more meaningful by striking a more contemporary note.

The Vicks story shows that a focus on the particular brings business rewards. But there are also psychic rewards for the manager who invests in the local. Going back to my roots reinvigorated me as a person and brought a certain fullness to my life. Not only was it pleasant to see familiar brown faces on the street, it also was enormously satisfying to be a part of the intense social life of the neighborhood, to experience the joys and sorrows of politics, and to share in the common fate of the nation. But at another level I also began to think of my work as a part of nation building, especially training and developing the next generation of young managers who would run the company and the country. It discharged a debt to my tutor at Harvard and a responsibility that we all have to the future.

Equally, it seems to me, there are powerful though less obvious psychic rewards for an international manager on transfer overseas who chooses to get involved in the local community. When such people approach the new country with an open mind, learn the local language, and make friends with colleagues and neighbors, they gain access to the wealth of a new culture. Not only will they be more effective as managers, they also will live fuller, richer lives.

Unfortunately, my experience in Mexico indicates that many expatriate managers live in "golden ghettos" of ease with little genuine contact with locals other than servants. Is it any surprise that they become isolated and complain of rootlessness and alienation in their new environment? The lesson for global companies is to give each international manager a local "mentor" who will open doors to the community. Ultimately, however, it is the responsibility of individual managers to open their minds, plunge into their local communities, and try to make them their own.

On Global Thinking

It would be wrong to conclude from the Vicks story that managing a global brand is purely a local affair. On the contrary, the winners in the new borderless economy will be the brands and companies that make best use of the richness of experience they get from their geographical diversity. Multinational companies have a natural advantage over local companies because they have talented people solving similar problems for identical brands in different parts of the world, and these brand managers can learn from each other's successes and failures. If a good idea emerges in Egypt, a smart brand manager in Malaysia or Venezuela will at least give it a test.

The Surat lady's teakettle became the basis of a national campaign in India. "One-pointedness" emerged from a hole-in-the-wall in Bombay, but it became the fulcrum on which we built a world-class business over a generation. Advertising for colds during the hot monsoon months seems highly parochial, but it taught us the importance of advertising year round in other places. The stockist system found applicability in Indonesia and China. Even the strange Ayurvedic system of medicine might plausibly be reapplied in the form of efficacious herbal remedies for common ailments in Western countries.

Business truths are invariably local in origin, but they are often expressions of fundamental human needs that are the same worldwide. Local insights with a universal character thus can become quickly global—though only in the hands of flexible, open-minded managers who can translate such ideas into new circumstances with sensitivity and understanding. My admonition to think local is only half the answer. Managers also must remember to think global. The insights we glean from each microcosm are ultimately universal.

Organizational specialists often express a fear that companies will demotivate their local managers by asking them to execute standardized global marketing packages. If they impose these standardized marketing solutions too rigidly, then this fear may be justified. However, this does not happen in successful companies. In fact, the more common disease in a global company is the "not invented here" syndrome, which especially afflicts subsidiaries and managers whose local triumphs have left them arrogant and unwilling to learn from successes in other parts of the world.

We in India were no different. But slowly and painfully we learned that useful lessons can emerge anywhere. For all our efforts to tap into the roots of Indian pluralism, we were dealing with a global brand. The product itself, the positioning, and the packaging were basically the same everywhere. Global brands are not free-for-alls, with each subsidiary doing its own thing. It took us six months, for example, to persuade our marketing people to try a new advertising idea for Vaporub that came from Mexico. It asked the consumer to use Vaporub on three parts of the body to obtain three types of relief. When we finally tried "Three-by-Three" in our advertising, it worked brilliantly.

It is deeply wrong to believe that going global is a one-stop, packaged decision. Local managers can add enormous value as they tap into local roots for insights. But it is equally wrong to neglect the integrity of the brand's core elements. Smart global managers nourish each blade of grass without neglecting the garden as a whole.

On Karma

Although the principles of managing a business in the Third World are the same as in the West, there are still big differences between the two. For me, the greatest of these is the pervasive reality of poverty.

I have lost the towering confidence of my youth, when I believed that socialism could wipe away poverty. The problem of socialism is one of performance, not vision. If it worked, we would all be socialists. Ironically, the legacy of the collectivist bias in Indian thinking has been the perpetuation of poverty. We created an over-regulated private sector and an inefficient public sector. We did not allow the economy to grow and produce the surplus that might have paid for direct poverty programs. We created an exploitative bureaucracy that fed on itself. Today, happily, we are righting the balance by liberalizing the economy, reducing state control, and restoring legitimacy to the market. I am confident that these changes will foster the entrepreneurialism and economic vitality India needs to create prosperity and eliminate the destitution of so many of its people.

Despite the problems, I find managers in India and other poor countries more optimistic than their counterparts in rich nations. The reason is that we believe our children will be better off than our parents were, and this idea is a great source of strength. We see our managerial work as nation building. We are the benign harbingers of technology and modernity. As we learn to manage complex enterprises, we empower people with the confidence they need to become responsible, innovative, and self-reliant.

It seems to come down to commitment. In committing to our work we commit to a here and now, to a particular place and time. The meaning in our lives comes from nourishing a particular blade of grass. It comes from absorbing ourselves so deeply in the microcosm of our work that we forget ourselves, especially our egos. The difference between subject and object disappears.

The Sanskrit phrase *nishkama karma* describes this state of utter absorption, in which people act for the sake of the action, not for the sake of the reward from the action. This is also the meaning of happiness.

Originally published in March–April 1993
Reprint 93202

Managing Risk
in an Unstable World

IAN BREMMER

Executive Summary

WITH EMERGING MARKETS like China and politically
unstable countries like Saudi Arabia figuring more than
ever into companies' investment calculations, business
leaders are turning to political risk analysis to measure
the impact of politics on potential markets, minimize risks,
and make the most of global opportunities. But political
risk is more subjective than its economic counterpart. It is
influenced by the passage of laws, the foibles of government leaders, and the rise of popular movements. So corporate leaders must grapple not just with broad, easily
observable trends but also with nuances of society and
even quirks of personality. And those hard-to-quantify factors must constantly be pieced together into an ongoing
narrative within historical and regional contexts.

As goods, services, information, ideas, and people
cross borders today with unprecedented velocity,

corporations debating operational or infrastructural investments abroad increasingly need objective, rigorous assessments. One tool for measuring and presenting stability data, for example, incorporates 20 composite indicators of risk in emerging markets and scores risk variables according to both their structural and their temporal components. The indicators are then organized into four equally weighted subcategories whose ratings are aggregated into a single stability score. Countries are ranked on a scale of zero (a failed state) to 100 (a fully institutionalized, stable democracy).

Companies can buy political risk analyses from consultants or, as some large energy and financial services organizations have done, develop them in-house. Either way, a complete and accurate picture of any country's risk requires analysts with strong reportorial skills; timely, accurate data on a variety of social and political trends; and a framework for evaluating the impact of individual risks on stability.

COUNTRIES IN TURMOIL elbow one another off the front page at a dizzying pace: Lebanon follows Ukraine follows Sudan follows Argentina. Companies, meanwhile, fear unpredictable change, even as they seek profit from the opportunities change creates—a freshly privatized industry in Turkey, recently tendered oil blocks in Libya, a new pro-Western government in the former Soviet republic of Ukraine. To help weigh dangers against opportunities, corporations mulling foreign ventures routinely consult economic risk analysts. But basing global investment decisions on economic data without understanding the political context is like basing nutrition decisions on calorie counts without examining the list of ingredients.

Reassuring data on countries' per capita income, growth, and inflation—the bread and butter of economic risk analysis—often obscures potential threats from other sources. Iran's parliament, for example, last year passed legislation that complicates foreign companies' abilities to plant stakes in that country's telecom sector. The 2003 revolution in Georgia altered the strategic calculus for investment in Caspian Sea energy development. The Kremlin's politically motivated prosecution of business tycoon Mikhail Khodorkovsky sent a chill through Russia's oil market. And Brazil's government is pressing both its agencies and its citizens to adopt open-source software, a policy that could inflict some nasty wounds on Microsoft and other technology companies.

These are examples of *political risk,* broadly defined as the impact of politics on markets. Political risk is influenced by the passage of laws, the foibles of leaders, and the rise of popular movements—in short, all the factors that might politically stabilize or destabilize a country. The significance of any given risk, of course, depends upon the context of the investment decision. A hedge fund manager worries about developments that could move markets tomorrow, while the leader of a corporation building an overseas chemical plant needs a longer view. Strategists evaluating emerging markets must be especially vigilant (in fact, an emerging market may be defined as a state in which politics matters at least as much as economics). But even those businesses active only in developed nations should factor political risk into their planning scenarios.

Most companies are already navigating the choppy waters of globalization, and none, presumably, are sailing blind. But corporate leaders may lack the sophisticated understanding this very complex subject requires. Political risk analysis is more subjective than its economic counterpart and demands that leaders grapple not just with broad, easily observable trends but also with nuances of society and even quirks of personality. And those hard-to-quantify factors must constantly be pieced into an ongoing narrative within historical and regional contexts.

This article will help corporate leaders become better appraisers of information about the myriad shifting influences on global investments. Armed with that understanding, business strategists can minimize risks and seize opportunities far beyond their home shores.

Politics Is Everyone's Business

Corporations with investments in such opaque countries as Zimbabwe, Myanmar, and Vietnam have long understood how political risk affects their bottom lines. In fact, historically, some of the business world's best political risk analysis has come from multinational corporations, like Royal Dutch/Shell and American International Group (AIG), that have entire departments dedicated to the subject. But today, any company with exposure in foreign markets needs early, accurate information on political developments. There are four principle reasons for this.

First, international markets are more interconnected than ever before. Tremors following a market shock in Argentina are quickly felt in Brazil and Venezuela, but they also rumble through Thailand. In 1997, capital flight from Southeast Asia roiled markets around the world. If

China's rapidly growing economy overshoots a soft landing and crashes into recession, the impact on Chile, Russia, India, and the United States will be measurable within hours. China's political decisions today will have dramatic long-term effects on its markets. Companies with exposure anywhere in the world that China does business ignore those decisions at their peril.

Second, for good or ill, the United States is making the world a more volatile place, and that has changed risk calculations everywhere. The attacks on the World Trade Center in New York put foreign affairs and security front and center of federal government policy. Washington has shown its willingness to aggressively preempt threats to American security and national interests. The U.S. military has demonstrated an unprecedented capability to respond to international shocks—and to create them.

Third, the offshoring trend is growing. Businesses shift some operations to countries where labor is cheap—but the labor is cheap for a reason. In countries such as India (an established offshoring destination) and Kenya (an emerging one), living conditions for the working classes can be harsh, and there is greater threat of unrest than in developed countries with their large, relatively prosperous middle classes. Offshoring presents other risks as well. The Chinese government, for example, is already cavalier about intellectual property rights and shows signs of becoming more so. Companies moving manufacturing and other functions there may be hard-pressed to protect some of their most valuable intellectual assets.

Fourth, the world is increasingly dependent for energy on states troubled by considerable political risk—Saudi Arabia, Iran, Nigeria, Russia, and Venezuela among them. As global supply struggles to keep pace with rising demand, political instability in these oil-producing states can quickly produce shocks all over the world.

It is difficult to imagine a business that is not affected by at least one or two of these developments. And corporations' exposure will only grow as supply chains become more global and developing countries increasingly participate in international trade.

What Economics Can't Tell You

Economic risk analysis and political risk analysis address two fundamentally different questions. Economic risk analysis tells corporate leaders whether a particular country *can* pay its debt. Political risk analysis tells them whether that country *will* pay its debt. Two examples illustrate this distinction.

When 35-year-old Sergei Kiriyenko replaced Viktor Chernomyrdin as prime minister in March 1998, Russia's economy seemed to be emerging from post–Soviet era turmoil. Inflation had been reduced to single digits, the economy was growing, and the government appeared committed to a moderate reformist path. Economic analysts saw clear skies.

But political analysts recognized that an obstructionist parliament intended to block Kremlin attempts to tighten fiscal policy and streamline tax collection. They saw that an absence of consensus was producing incoherent monetary policies and that the absentee, alcoholic president wasn't going to enforce discipline on an increasingly chaotic policy-formulation process. When oil prices fell, political analysts underlined the country's lack of fiscal discipline as a cause for immediate concern.

In short, political analysts produced a darker—and more accurate—portrait of Russia's market instability in the period leading up to the financial crisis of 1998. When Russia ultimately defaulted on international debt and devalued the ruble, companies that had studied both economic and political risk weathered the storm with far fewer repercussions than those that had relied on economic analysis alone.

In other instances, political risk analysts have been able to detect the silver linings in economists' dark clouds. The value of Brazilian bonds and currency fell sharply in 2002 when it became clear that Luis Inacio Lula da Silva would be elected that country's president. In earlier campaigns, Lula had criticized the International Monetary Fund and Brazil's fiscal conservatives, whom he accused of widening the gap between rich and poor. Comparisons of Lula with Cuba's Fidel Castro and Venezuelan president Hugo Chávez spooked economic risk analysts, who feared that the election of Brazil's first "leftist" president would produce a politically driven market crisis.

But many political analysts considered such an outcome unlikely. In Lula they saw not an ideologue or a theoretician but a man who made his name as a tough, pragmatic labor negotiator. They observed in his campaign an inclusive, conciliatory electoral strategy. They heard in his speeches a determination not to allow Brazil to fall into the kind of financial crisis that had inflicted so much damage on Argentina. And so they argued that Lula's victory would be more likely to produce political and economic stability. If Lula won, they predicted, his government would enfranchise the poor. And he would keep his campaign promise to reserve an IMF-established percentage of tax revenue for the repayment of debt, instead of spending it on social programs and make-work projects.

The political analysts were right. Lula won the election and kept his promises of fiscal discipline. Within weeks, Brazilian bonds staged a dramatic recovery.

Strength Against Shocks

In both Russia and Brazil, political analysts focused on how a specific leadership change would affect the country's *stability*—the unit of measure for political risk. A nation's stability is determined by two things: political leaders' capacity to implement the policies they want even amidst shocks and their ability to avoid generating shocks of their own. A country with both capabilities will always be more stable than a country with just one. Countries with neither are the most vulnerable to political risk.

Shocks themselves are another important concept in political risk. They can be either internal (demonstrations in Egypt; a transfer of political power in Cuba) or external (thousands of refugees fleeing from North Korea into China; the tsunami in Southeast Asia). The presence of shocks alone, however, is not a sign of instability. Saudi Arabia, for example, has produced countless shocks over the years but has so far ridden out the tremors. It will probably continue to do so, at least in the near term: The nation is built on political and religious fault lines, but its strong authoritarian control and deep pockets allow the Saudi elite to adapt to quite dramatic changes.

Saudi Arabia's relative stability is grounded in its capacity to withstand shocks; other countries depend more on their capacity not to produce them. Kazakhstan's political structure, for example, is less supple and adaptable than that of Saudi Arabia. But the country also stands much further from the epicenter of political earthquakes.

Clearly then, two countries will react differently to similar shocks, depending on how stable they are. Say an election is held and a head of state is chosen but the victory is challenged by a large number of voters, and the nation's highest judicial body must rule on a recount. That happened in the United States in 2000 without any significant implications for the stability of the country or its markets. When similar events erupted in Taiwan in 2003 and Ukraine in 2004, however, demonstrations closed city streets, civil violence threatened, and international observers speculated on the viability of those nations' economies.

The 2000 U.S. elections point to another complicating factor in political risk: the relationship between stability and openness. The United States is stable because it is open—information flows widely, people express themselves freely, and institutions matter more than personalities. Consequently, the nation weathered its election controversy without a Wall Street panic; investors knew the problem would be resolved and that the outcome would be broadly perceived as legitimate.

But other countries—such as North Korea, Myanmar, and Cuba—are stable because they are closed. What's more, the slightest opening could push the most brittle of these nations into dangerous territory. Twenty minutes' exposure to CNN would reveal to North Korean citizens how outrageously their government lies to them about life outside; the result might be significant unrest. And while there is considerable world pressure on closed countries to open up, the transition from a stable-because-closed state to a stable-because-open state is inevitably marked by instability. Some nations, for instance South Africa, survive that transition. Others, like the Soviet Union, collapse.

Plotting where nations lie on the openness-stability spectrum, and in which direction they are heading, is tricky. And no country poses a greater challenge than China, which appears equally at home on two different points along this range. Politically, China is stable-because-closed; it is a police state with absolute control over public expression. For example, security forces severely restricted media coverage of the recent death of Zhao Ziyang, a relatively progressive politician, in order to prevent the kinds of uprisings sparked by the deaths of Chou En-lai in 1976 and Hu Yaobang in 1989. Economically, however, China is opening at a rapid clip, as diplomats and negotiators globe trot in search of new trade relationships to feed the country's growth.

When a country is politically closed but economically open, something has to give. Whether China's political system will follow its economic trend line or vice versa is a fascinating and hotly contested subject in the political analyst community. (See "Why China Keeps Us Up at Night" at the end of this article.)

Corporate executives, however, generally focus on more immediate concerns when assessing a country's ripeness for investment. Broadly speaking, decision makers must know three things: How likely is it that a shock will occur? If likely, when will it probably occur? And how high are the stakes if it does?

The greatest risk, not surprisingly, is when shocks are likely, imminent, and have widespread consequences. All three conditions exist in North Korea, which has remained stable only by resisting movement toward market economics and more open government. North Korea's stability is so dependent on Kim Jong Il and the country's military elite that any threat to their safety could destroy the regime and destabilize the entire region very quickly. And the stakes are high because the most valuable products North Korea has to sell—military and nuclear components—tend to produce political shocks.

In other nations, shocks are likely and expected to occur relatively soon, but the stakes for world markets are much lower. Fidel Castro, for example, is 78, and the fate of the revolution after his death is unclear. Castro's hard-line younger brother Raul might assume power, but he is also in his 70s; if he replaces Castro, political uncertainty will build until the next transfer of power. Similarly, if a reformer like Carlos Lage steps forward to begin a process of gradual opening, the release of long-repressed dissent could spark violence. So either outcome will probably produce instability. But because Cuba is not an exporter of nuclear technology, oil, or any other vital resource, the shock's effect on world markets will be minor.

Risk by the Numbers

Speculation on the outcomes of these and other scenarios appears in numerous publications, but corporations debating operational or infrastructure investments abroad need more objective, rigorous assessments than those found in the op-ed pages. Companies can either buy political risk services from consultants or, like Shell and AIG, develop the capacity in-house. Either way, a complete and accurate picture of any country's risk requires analysts with strong reportorial skills; timely, accurate data on a variety of social and political trends; and a framework for evaluating the impact of individual risks on stability.

THE ANALYSTS

Politics never stops moving, and risk analysts must be able to follow a nation's story as it develops. Usually, that means being on the ground in that country. And in the case of a particularly opaque regime, it can mean being there a very long time. Some information is published in official reports or in the media, but analysts will gather most of their intelligence from primary sources: well-connected journalists in the local and foreign press, current and former midlevel officials, and think tank specialists.

Companies should bear in mind that political analysis is more subjective and consequently more vulnerable to bias than its economic counterpart. One danger is that analysts with their own political opinions may view their research through a particular philosophical scrim. In addition, political analysts will probably have subject-matter—as well as nation-specific—expertise that can color their reports. A Taiwan analyst with a background in security, for example, may overemphasize such risk variables as cross-strait tensions and the growing imbalance of military power between Taiwan and China. An Eastern Europe analyst studying social unrest may insist that demonstrations by pensioners have the largest political impact on the government. As decision makers peruse analysts' reports, they should be alert for any potential bias and correct for it.

THE DATA

Because of their very nature, political risk variables are more difficult to measure than economic variables (although in some countries, such as China and Saudi Arabia, even the reliability of government-produced economic data is open to question). Politics, after all, is influenced by human behavior and the sudden confluence of events, for which no direct calibrations exist. How do you assign numbers to such concepts as the rule of law?

To accurately quantify political risk, then, analysts need proxies for their variables. Instead of trying to measure the independence of a nation's judiciary, for example, analysts can determine whether judges in a particular country are paid a living wage, whether funded programs exist to inform them about new legislation, and whether—and how often—they are targeted for assassination. Political risk analysts also study the percentage of children who regularly attend school, how police and military salaries compare with criminal opportunities, and how much access to medical care is available in towns with populations of 10,000 to 50,000 people. They look at such statistics as the unemployment rate for people between the ages of 18 and 29 and determine how many of them are in prison. And, of course, they add economic variables to the mix: per capita income, balance of payments, and national debt.

Taken together, this often anecdotal information reveals much about a country's underlying sources of strength or vulnerability. Comparing data from neighboring countries provides a good sense of where shocks from unstable nations might rumble into stable ones. Comparing a single nation's data points over time tells the analyst whether that nation is becoming more stable or less so, and how quickly.

THE FRAMEWORK

Different companies and consultancies will have different methods for measuring and presenting stability data. We at Eurasia Group have developed a tool that incorporates 20 composite indicators of risk in emerging markets. Distributed as part of a strategic relationship with Deutsche Bank, the Deutsche Bank Eurasia Group Stability Index (DESIX) scores risk variables according to both their structural and temporal components. Structural scores highlight long-term underlying conditions that affect stability. They then serve as a baseline for temporal scores, which reflect the impact of policies, events, and developments that occur each month.

The indicators are organized into four equally weighted subcategories: government, society, security, and the economy. Ratings for all four subcategories are aggregated into a single composite stability rating, which is expressed as a number on a scale of zero to 100—from a failed state to a fully institutionalized, stable democracy. (See the exhibits "Political Risk at a Glance" and "Anatomy of India's Political Risk.")

Very often, the numbers that make up the stability rating are as interesting as the stability rating itself. Consider Turkey, whose March 2005 stability rating was 60, five points lower than Brazil's and two points higher than Russia's. Within that composite number, components are moving in opposite directions.

Specifically, Turkey's government rating rose as a consequence of the European Union agreement to open accession talks with Ankara in October 2005. Prime Minister Recep Tayyip Erdogan's administration now has greater incentive to continue reforms that strengthen the independence of Turkey's institutions, increase media freedom, and protect the rights of minority groups—such as Turkish Kurds—who might otherwise provoke unrest. Turkish membership in the EU would also bind the country more closely to European institutions, further increasing stability.

Political Risk at a Glance

Political risk measures the stability of individual countries based on factors grounded in government, society, security, and the economy. Emerging markets are generally in the moderate- to high-stability range.

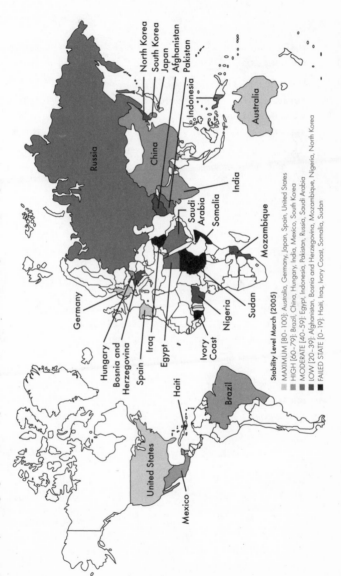

Stability Level March (2005)

MAXIMUM [80–100]: Australia, Germany, Japan, Spain, United States

HIGH [60–79]: Brazil, China, Hungary, India, Mexico, South Korea

MODERATE [40–59]: Egypt, Indonesia, Pakistan, Russia, Saudi Arabia

LOW [20–39]: Afghanistan, Bosnia and Herzegovina, Mozambique, Nigeria, North Korea

FAILED STATE [0–19]: Haiti, Iraq, Ivory Coast, Somalia, Sudan

Anatomy of India's Political Risk

National stability scores are plotted over time and comprise dozens of measurements, ranging from hard economic data on growth and investment to more amorphous assessments of youth disaffection and corruption. At the beginning of this year, India was hovering between moderate and high stability. (The numbers used to obtain each average have been rounded off.)

Factors affecting stability	Stability scores (0 –100)			Comments
	Jan 2005	Feb 2005	Mar 2005	
Government (such as strength of current government, rule of law, and level of corruption)	67	64	62	Political missteps by the government led to poor performance in state elections and strengthened opposition parties.
Society (such as social tension, youth disaffection, and health, education, and other services)	58	58	58	Low per capita income and literacy levels lead to a low human development index. Simmering social tensions keep the society score low.
Security (such as level of globalization, geostrategic condition, and emergencies and disasters)	53	48	48	Peace talks with Pakistan and China have eased security fears. But a Maoist insurgency in Nepal and continuing Kashmir violence keep the score low.
Economy (such as fiscal condition, growth and investment, and external sector and debt)	75	75	76	Economic growth and expanding trade keep the numbers healthy. The fiscal deficit remains a worry.
Cumulative National Stability Score	**63**	**61**	**62**	

Source: Deutsche Bank Eurasia Group Stability Index (DESIX), March 2005.

Yet Turkey's security rating is pushed lower by the continued presence of Kurdistan Workers' Party militants in northern Iraq. Ankara worries that the Kurds—empowered by the Iraqi elections—may try to regain control of the oil-rich northern Iraqi town of Kirkuk, which would provide the financial basis for an independent Kurdish state. A Kurdish state on Turkey's borders would likely fan separatist flames in that country's own Kurdish population.

Once You Know the Odds

How companies apply such analysis obviously depends upon their industry, strategy, and risk tolerance profile. Of necessity, companies in the energy industry, for example, have demonstrated a high tolerance for risk, relying on mitigation techniques to manage their exposure. By contrast, light manufacturers and midsize companies in industrial supply chains tend to bide their time to see how situations evolve. And pharmaceutical corporations generally shy away from investment when presented with infrastructure or intellectual property risks.

Companies making extended commitments in unstable nations must give top priority to long-term risk—issues related to demographics and natural resources, for example—when making decisions. In May 2004, Japan's Sumitomo Chemical agreed to a $4.3 billion joint venture with Saudi Aramco to build a major petrochemical plant at Rabigh in Saudi Arabia. The plant isn't scheduled to open until 2008, so Sumitomo is particularly vulnerable to such pernicious demographic trends as the exodus of technical talent and the joblessness of young men.

Sumitomo's risk tolerance is already being tested by an Islamic extremist campaign of kidnapping and beheading foreigners who do business in the country.

But while violence and corruption dominate headlines, such near-term risks are much exaggerated. (See "Why Saudi Arabia Keeps Us Up at Night" at the end of this article.) In fact, although Saudi Arabia—and China, too—may be risky bets for companies engaged in ventures that won't see profitability for a decade, in the short run there is money to be made. Among others, General Motors, Kodak, and a number of investment banks have already done so—though they've stumbled a bit in the process.

Once companies have determined that a particular investment is worth the danger, they can use traditional techniques to mitigate the risk—recruiting local partners, for example, or limiting R&D in nations with leaky intellectual property protection. In addition, a growing number of commercial and government organizations now offer insurance against political risks such as the expropriation of property, political violence, currency inconvertibility, and breach of contract. (Such insurance is expensive, however, because risks are so hard to assess.) Otherwise it's mostly a matter of hedging—locating a factory in Mexico as well as Venezuela, say, so as not to bet the entire Latin America strategy on a single opaque regime.

Finally, it is worth remembering that though instability translates into greater risk, risk is not always a bad thing. Political risk in underdeveloped countries nearly always carries an upside because such nations are so unstable that negative shocks can do little further damage. On the stability ladder, for example, Afghanistan and Cambodia simply don't have far to fall; only favorable external conditions—such as debt relief from the developed world or loans from international institutions—could have much effect on their political stability. For some companies, that could make investments in such countries an attractive part of an enterprise risk portfolio.

Politics has always been inseparable from markets; the world's first transnational trade organizations were moved by the political waves of their time. Today, goods, services, information, ideas, and people cross borders with unprecedented velocity—and the trend is only intensifying. For company leaders seeking profit in places that are socially, culturally, and governmentally alien, the complementary insights of political and economic risk analysts are vital.

Why China Keeps Us Up at Night

CHINA BESTRIDES the world of political risk like a colossus. Many experts tout it as the great investment opportunity of the new millennium, but it is also a great unknown. Among the questions political risk analysts are studying: Can China's explosive economic growth survive its corrupt and inefficient political system? Do the country's political leaders agree that preparations for a soft landing to avoid recession are necessary? Would reform that opens its political process make China more stable or less?

China's continued expansion depends on the central government's capacity to handle complex economic transitions and avoid instability. At the same time, the state must juggle huge security, demographic, and political challenges. Imminent agricultural, banking, and urban policy reforms will probably produce even more complex management problems for the country's dysfunctional bureaucracy.

China appears to be inching toward instability as reforms strain the relationships between national and regional leaders, increasing the probability of an economic shock followed by a political one. Complicating matters, China's bureaucracy lacks the administrative control necessary to modulate the pace of an economic slowdown.

Analysts of economic risk tend to base projections for China's growth rates on its past performance. But there are few countries for which past performance is so poor a predictor of future results. With a few notable exceptions, such as the 1989 protests in Tiananmen Square, social unrest in modern-day China has been rare. But the risk of popular unrest is going up as a result of widening income inequality, slowing—although still intense—economic growth, and continuing official abuse and corruption. The urban unemployed and migrant workers could stage protests; rural rebellion over land reclamations and onerous administrative fees could escalate. China's leaders might then clamp down on the media, religious groups, use of the Internet, and other forms of expression and communication. Faced with international criticism, the government could become more antagonistic and dogmatic about issues of concern to the United States and East Asia.

The probability of such events occurring in the short-term is low, but China's risk indicators suggest it is rising.

Why Saudi Arabia Keeps Us Up at Night

SAUDI ARABIA'S STABILITY is under fire from religious and secular forces. Islamic extremists hope to undermine the legitimacy of the royal family. Real unemployment is estimated to be between 20% and 25%; frustrated, job-less young men are flocking to mosques and schools where religious leaders thunder against the infidels. Western nations, meanwhile, are calling on the royals to move toward political liberalization. And the flight of expatriates will eventually take its toll on the Saudis' ability to diversify their economy.

Such volatility complicates financial deals—particularly those that take years to assemble—and extends the exposure to political risk over time.

But while companies with long-term investments must worry, short-term investors in Saudi Arabia have less cause for concern. That's because oil money stabilizes the political system, and the royal family can count on those revenues for years to come. Yes, oil supplies are a tempting target for terrorists; but the country's oil infrastructure is isolated from population centers, and redundancies in the pipeline system make it almost impossible to inflict lasting damage with a single blow. In addition, the national oil company has the technology, the trained engineers, and the spare capacity to continue producing significantly more than 9 million barrels per day. Finally, in light of concerns that foreign governments might freeze Saudi assets following September 11, 2001, a great deal of money flowed back into the kingdom, providing the House of Saud with more ready cash.

Clearly, any project in Saudi Arabia that needs a decade to show a profit is deeply problematic. But those willing to brave volatility in the near term may profit from opportunities that more risk-averse companies forgo.

Originally published in June 2005
Reprint R0506B

Serving the World's Poor, Profitably

C. K. PRAHALAD AND ALLEN HAMMOND

Executive Summary

BY STIMULATING COMMERCE and development at the bottom of the economic pyramid, multinationals could radically improve the lives of billions of people and help create a more stable, less dangerous world. Achieving this goal does not require MNCs to spearhead global social-development initiatives for charitable purposes. They need only act in their own self-interest. How? The authors lay out the business case for entering the world's poorest markets.

Fully 65% of the world's population earns less than $2,000 per year—that's 4 billion people. But despite the vastness of this market, it remains largely untapped. The reluctance to invest is easy to understand, but it is, by and large, based on outdated assumptions of the developing world.

While individual incomes may be low, the aggregate buying power of poor communities is actually quite large, representing a substantial market in many countries for what some might consider luxury goods like satellite television and phone services. Prices, and margins, are often much higher in poor neighborhoods than in their middle-class counterparts. And new technologies are already steadily reducing the effects of corruption, illiteracy, inadequate infrastructure, and other such barriers.

Because these markets are in the earliest stages of economic development, revenue growth for multinationals entering them can be extremely rapid. MNCs can also lower costs, not only through low-cost labor but by transferring operating efficiencies and innovations developed to serve their existing operations.

Certainly, succeeding in such markets requires MNCs to think creatively. The biggest change, though, has to come from executives: Unless business leaders confront their own preconceptions—particularly about the value of high-volume, low-margin businesses—companies are unlikely to master the challenges or reap the rewards of these developing markets.

CONSIDER THIS BLEAK VISION of the world 15 years from now: The global economy recovers from its current stagnation but growth remains anemic. Deflation continues to threaten, the gap between rich and poor keeps widening, and incidents of economic chaos, governmental collapse, and civil war plague developing regions. Terrorism remains a constant threat, diverting significant public and private resources to security concerns. Opposition to the global market system intensifies. Multinational companies find it difficult to expand, and many become risk averse, slowing investment and pulling back from emerging markets.

Now consider this much brighter scenario: Driven by private investment and widespread entrepreneurial activity, the economies of developing regions grow vigorously, creating jobs and wealth and bringing hundreds of millions of new consumers into the global marketplace every year. China, India, Brazil, and, gradually, South Africa become new engines of global economic growth, promoting prosperity around the world. The resulting decrease in poverty produces a range of social benefits, helping to stabilize many developing regions and reduce civil and cross-border conflicts. The threat of terrorism and war recedes. Multinational companies expand rapidly in an era of intense innovation and competition.

Both of these scenarios are possible. Which one comes to pass will be determined primarily by one factor: the willingness of big, multinational companies to enter and invest in the world's poorest markets. By stimulating commerce and development at the bottom of the economic pyramid, MNCs could radically improve the lives of billions of people and help bring into being a more stable, less dangerous world. Achieving this goal does not require multinationals to spearhead global social development initiatives for charitable purposes. They need only act in their own self-interest, for there are enormous business benefits to be gained by entering developing markets. In fact, many innovative companies—entrepreneurial outfits and large, established enterprises alike—are already serving the world's poor in ways that generate strong revenues, lead to greater operating efficiencies, and uncover new sources of innovation. For these companies—and those that follow their lead—building businesses aimed at the bottom of the pyramid promises to provide important competitive advantages as the twenty-first century unfolds.

Big companies are not going to solve the economic ills of developing countries by themselves, of course. It will also take targeted financial aid from the developed world and improvements in the governance of the developing nations themselves. But it's clear to us that prosperity can come to the poorest regions only through the direct and sustained involvement of multinational companies. And it's equally clear that the multinationals can enhance their own prosperity in the process.

Untapped Potential

Everyone knows that the world's poor are distressingly plentiful. Fully 65% of the world's population earns less than $2,000 each per year—that's 4 billion people. But despite the vastness of this market, it remains largely untapped by multinational companies. The reluctance to invest is easy to understand. Companies assume that people with such low incomes have little to spend on goods and services and that what they do spend goes to basic needs like food and shelter. They also assume that various barriers to commerce—corruption, illiteracy, inadequate infrastructure, currency fluctuations, bureaucratic red tape—make it impossible to do business profitably in these regions. (See the exhibit "The World Pyramid.")

But such assumptions reflect a narrow and largely outdated view of the developing world. The fact is, many multinationals already successfully do business in developing countries (although most currently focus on selling to the small upper-middle-class segments of these markets), and their experience shows that the barriers to commerce—although real—are much lower than is typically thought. Moreover, several positive trends in developing countries—from political reform, to a growing openness to investment, to the development of low-cost wireless communication networks—are reducing the barriers further while also providing businesses with greater access to even the poorest city slums and rural areas. Indeed, once the misperceptions are wiped away, the enormous economic potential that lies at the bottom of the pyramid becomes clear.

Take the assumption that the poor have no money. It sounds obvious on the surface, but it's wrong. While individual incomes may be low, the aggregate buying power of poor communities is actually quite large. The average per capita income of villagers in rural

The World Pyramid

Most companies target consumers at the upper tiers of the economic pyramid, completely overlooking the business potential at its base. But though they may each be earning the equivalent of less than $2,000 a year, the people at the bottom of the pyramid make up a colossal market—4 billion strong—the vast majority of the world's population.

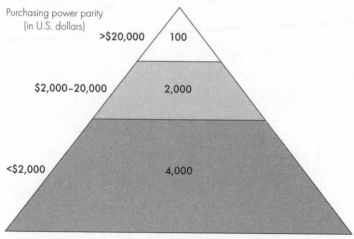

Purchasing power parity (in U.S. dollars)

>$20,000   100

$2,000–20,000   2,000

<$2,000   4,000

Population (in millions)

Bangladesh, for instance, is less than $200 per year, but as a group they are avid consumers of telecommunications services. Grameen Telecom's village phones, which are owned by a single entrepreneur but used by the entire community, generate an average revenue of roughly $90 a month—and as much as $1,000 a month in some large villages. Customers of these village phones, who pay cash for each use, spend an average of 7% of their income on phone services—a far higher percentage than consumers in traditional markets do.

It's also incorrect to assume that the poor are too concerned with fulfilling their basic needs to "waste" money on nonessential goods. In fact, the poor often do buy "luxury" items. In the Mumbai shantytown of Dharavi, for example, 85% of households own a television set, 75% own a pressure cooker and a mixer, 56% own a gas stove, and 21% have telephones. That's because buying a house in Mumbai, for most people at the bottom of the pyramid, is not a realistic option. Neither is getting access to running water. They accept that reality, and rather than saving for a rainy day, they spend their income on things they can get now that improve the quality of their lives.

Another big misperception about developing markets is that the goods sold there are incredibly cheap and, hence, there's no room for a new competitor to come in and turn a profit. In reality, consumers at the bottom of the pyramid pay much higher prices for most things than middle-class consumers do, which means that there's a real opportunity for companies, particularly big corporations with economies of scale and efficient supply chains, to capture market share by offering higher quality goods at lower prices while maintaining attractive margins. In fact, throughout the developing world, urban slum dwellers pay, for instance, between four and 100 times as much for drinking water as middle- and upper-class families. Food also costs 20% to 30% more in the poorest communities since there is no access to bulk discount stores. On the service side of the economy, local money-lenders charge interest of 10% to 15% *per day,* with annual rates running as high as 2,000%. Even the lucky small-scale entrepreneurs who get loans from nonprofit microfinance institutions pay between 40% and 70% interest per year—rates that are illegal in most developed countries. (For a closer look at how the prices of goods compare in rich and poor areas, see the exhibit "The High-Cost Economy of the Poor.")

It can also be surprisingly cheap to market and deliver products and services to the world's poor. That's because many of them live in cities that are densely populated today and will be even more so in the years to come. Figures from the UN and the World Resources Institute indicate that by 2015, in Africa, 225 cities will each have populations of more than 1 million; in Latin America, another 225; and in Asia, 903. The population of at least 27 cities will reach or exceed 8 million. Collectively, the 1,300 largest cities will account for some 1.5 billion to 2 billion people, roughly half of whom will be bottom-of-the-pyramid (BOP) consumers now served primarily by informal economies. Companies that operate in these areas will have access to millions of potential new customers, who together have billions of dollars to spend. The poor in Rio de Janeiro, for instance, have a total purchasing power of $1.2 billion ($600 per person). Shanty-towns in Johannesburg or Mumbai are no different.

The slums of these cities already have distinct ecosystems, with retail shops, small businesses, schools, clinics, and moneylenders. Although there are few reliable estimates of the value of commercial transactions in slums, business activity appears to be thriving. Dharavi—covering an area of just 435 acres—boasts scores of businesses ranging from leather, textiles, plastic recycling, and surgical sutures to gold jewelry, illicit liquor, detergents, and groceries. The scale of the businesses varies from one-person operations to bigger, well-recognized producers of brand-name products. Dharavi generates an estimated $450 million in manufacturing revenues, or about $1 million per acre of land. Established shantytowns in São Paulo, Rio, and Mexico City are equally productive. The seeds of a vibrant commercial sector have been sown.

While the rural poor are naturally harder to reach than the urban poor, they also represent a large untapped

---

The High-Cost Economy of the Poor

When we compare the costs of essentials in Dharavi, a shantytown of more than 1 million people in the heart of Mumbai, India, with those of Warden Road, an upper-class community in a nice Mumbai suburb, a disturbing picture emerges. Clearly, costs could be dramatically reduced if the poor could benefit from the scope, scale, and supply-chain efficiencies of large enterprises, as their middle-class counterparts do. This pattern is common around the world, even in developed countries. For instance, a similar, if less exaggerated, disparity exists between the inner-city poor and the suburban rich in the United States.

Cost	Dharavi	Warden Road	Poverty Premium
Credit (annual interest)	600%–1,000%	12%–18%	53X
Municipal-grade water (per cubic meter)	$1.12	$0.03	37X
Phone call (per minute)	$0.04–$0.05	$0.025	1.8X
Diarrhea medication	$20	$2	10X
Rice (per kilogram)	$0.28	$0.24	1.2X

opportunity for companies. Indeed, 60% of India's GDP is generated in rural areas. The critical barrier to doing business in rural regions is distribution access, not a lack of buying power. But new information technology and communications infrastructures—especially wireless—promise to become an inexpensive way to establish marketing and distribution channels in these communities.

Conventional wisdom says that people in BOP markets cannot use such advanced technologies, but that's just another misconception. Poor rural women in Bangladesh have had no difficulty using GSM cell phones, despite never before using phones of any type. In Kenya, teenagers from slums are being successfully trained as Web page designers. Poor farmers in El Salvador use telecenters to negotiate the sale of their crops over the Internet. And women in Indian coastal villages have in less than a week learned to use PCs to interpret real-time satellite images showing concentrations of schools of fish in the Arabian Sea so they can direct their husbands to the best fishing areas. Clearly, poor communities are ready to adopt new technologies that improve their economic opportunities or their quality of life. The lesson for multinationals: Don't hesitate to deploy advanced technologies at the bottom of the pyramid while, or even before, deploying them in advanced countries.

A final misperception concerns the highly charged issue of exploitation of the poor by MNCs. The informal economies that now serve poor communities are full of inefficiencies and exploitive intermediaries. So if a microfinance institution charges 50% annual interest when the alternative is either 1,000% interest or no loan at all, is that exploiting or helping the poor? If a large financial company such as Citigroup were to use its scale to offer microloans at 20%, is that exploiting or helping

the poor? The issue is not just cost but also quality—
quality in the range and fairness of financial services,
quality of food, quality of water. We argue that when
MNCs provide basic goods and services that reduce costs
to the poor and help improve their standard of living—
while generating an acceptable return on investment—
the results benefit everyone.

The Business Case

The business opportunities at the bottom of the pyramid have not gone unnoticed. Over the last five years,
we have seen nongovernmental organizations (NGOs),
entrepreneurial start-ups, and a handful of forward-
thinking multinationals conduct vigorous commercial
experiments in poor communities. Their experience is a
proof of concept: Businesses can gain three important
advantages by serving the poor—a new source of revenue
growth, greater efficiency, and access to innovation. Let's
look at examples of each.

TOP-LINE GROWTH

Growth is an important challenge for every company, but
today it is especially critical for very large companies,
many of which appear to have nearly saturated their
existing markets. That's why BOP markets represent
such an opportunity for MNCs: They are fundamentally
new sources of growth. And because these markets are in
the earliest stages of economic development, growth can
be extremely rapid.

Latent demand for low-priced, high-quality goods is
enormous. Consider the reaction when Hindustan Lever,
the Indian subsidiary of Unilever, recently introduced

what was for it a new product category—candy—aimed at the bottom of the pyramid. A high-quality confection made with real sugar and fruit, the candy sells for only about a penny a serving. At such a price, it may seem like a marginal business opportunity, but in just six months it became the fastest-growing category in the company's portfolio. Not only is it profitable, but the company estimates it has the potential to generate revenues of $200 million per year in India and comparable markets in five years. Hindustan Lever has had similar successes in India with low-priced detergent and iodized salt. Beyond generating new sales, the company is establishing its business and its brand in a vast new market.

There is equally strong demand for affordable services. TARAhaat, a start-up focused on rural India, has introduced a range of computer-enabled education services ranging from basic IT training to English proficiency to vocational skills. The products are expected to be the largest single revenue generator for the company and its franchisees over the next several years.[1] Credit and financial services are also in high demand among the poor. Citibank's ATM-based banking experiment in India, called Suvidha, for instance, which requires a minimum deposit of just $25, enlisted 150,000 customers in one year in the city of Bangalore alone.

Small-business services are also popular in BOP markets. Centers run in Uganda by the Women's Information Resource Electronic Service (WIRES) provide female entrepreneurs with information on markets and prices, as well as credit and trade support services, packaged in simple, ready-to-use formats in local languages. The centers are planning to offer other small-business services such as printing, faxing, and copying, along with access to accounting, spreadsheet, and other software. In

Bolivia, a start-up has partnered with the Bolivian Association of Ecological Producers Organizations to offer business information and communications services to more than 25,000 small producers of ecoagricultural products.

It's true that some services simply cannot be offered at a low-enough cost to be profitable, at least not with traditional technologies or business models. Most mobile telecommunications providers, for example, cannot yet profitably operate their networks at affordable prices in the developing world. One answer is to find alternative technology. A microfinance organization in Bolivia named PRODEM, for example, uses multilingual smart-card ATMs to substantially reduce its marginal cost per customer. Smart cards store a customer's personal details, account numbers, transaction records, and a fingerprint, allowing cash dispensers to operate without permanent network connections—which is key in remote areas. What's more, the machines offer voice commands in Spanish and several local dialects and are equipped with touch screens so that PRODEM's customer base can be extended to illiterate and semiliterate people.

Another answer is to aggregate demand, making the community—not the individual—the network customer. Gyandoot, a start-up in the Dhar district of central India, where 60% of the population falls below the poverty level, illustrates the benefits of a shared access model. The company has a network of 39 Internet-enabled kiosks that provide local entrepreneurs with Internet and telecommunications access, as well as with governmental, educational, and other services. Each kiosk serves 25 to 30 surrounding villages; the entire network reaches more than 600 villages and over half a million people.

Networks like these can be useful channels for marketing and distributing many kinds of low-cost products and services. Aptech's Computer Education division, for example, has built its own network of 1,000 learning centers in India to market and distribute Vidya, a computer-training course specially designed for BOP consumers and available in seven Indian languages. Pioneer Hi-Bred, a DuPont company, uses Internet kiosks in Latin America to deliver agricultural information and to interact with customers. Farmers can report different crop diseases or weather conditions, receive advice over the wire, and order seeds, fertilizers, and pesticides. This network strategy increases both sales and customer loyalty.

REDUCED COSTS

No less important than top-line growth are cost-saving opportunities. Outsourcing operations to low-cost labor markets has, of course, long been a popular way to contain costs, and it has led to the increasing prominence of China in manufacturing and India in software. Now, thanks to the rapid expansion of high-speed digital networks, companies are realizing even greater savings by locating such labor-intensive service functions as call centers, marketing services, and back-office transaction processing in developing areas. For example, the nearly 20 companies that use OrphanIT.com's affiliate-marketing services, provided via its telecenters in India and the Philippines, pay one-tenth the going rate for similar services in the United States or Australia. Venture capitalist Vinod Khosla describes the remote-services opportunity this way: "I suspect that by 2010, we will be talking about [remote services] as the fastest-growing part of the world economy, with many trillions of dollars of new markets created." Besides keeping costs down, outsourcing jobs to BOP markets can enhance growth, since job creation ultimately increases local consumers' purchasing power.

But tapping into cheap labor pools is not the only way MNCs can enhance their efficiency by operating in developing regions. The competitive necessity of maintaining a low cost structure in these areas can push companies to discover creative ways to configure their products, finances, and supply chains to enhance productivity. And these discoveries can often be incorporated back into their existing operations in developed markets.

For instance, companies targeting the BOP market are finding that the shared access model, which disaggregates access from ownership, not only widens their customer base but increases asset productivity as well. Poor people, rather than buying their own computers, Internet connections, cell phones, refrigerators, and even cars, can use such equipment on a pay-per-use basis. Typically, the providers of such services get considerably more revenue per dollar of investment in the underlying assets. One shared Internet line, for example, can serve as many as 50 people, generating more revenue per day than if it were dedicated to a single customer at a flat fee. Shared access creates the opportunity to gain far greater returns from all sorts of infrastructure investments.

In terms of finances, to operate successfully in BOP markets, managers must also rethink their business metrics—specifically, the traditional focus on high gross margins. In developing markets, the profit margin on individual units will always be low. What really counts is capital efficiency—getting the highest possible returns on capital employed (ROCE). Hindustan Lever, for instance, operates a $2.6 billion business portfolio with zero working capital. The key is constant efforts to reduce capital investments by extensively outsourcing manufacturing, streamlining supply chains, actively managing receivables, and paying close attention to distributors' performance. Very low capital needs, focused distribution and technology investments, and very large volumes at low margins lead to very high ROCE businesses, creating great economic value for shareholders. It's a model that can be equally attractive in developed and developing markets.

Streamlining supply chains often involves replacing assets with information. Consider, for example, the experience of ITC, one of India's largest companies. Its agribusiness division has deployed a total of 970 kiosks serving 600,000 farmers who supply it with soy, coffee, shrimp, and wheat from 5,000 villages spread across India. This kiosk program, called e-Choupal, helps increase the farmers' productivity by disseminating the latest information on weather and best practices in farming, and by supporting other services like soil and water testing, thus facilitating the supply of quality inputs to both the farmers and ITC. The kiosks also serve as an e-procurement system, helping farmers earn higher prices by minimizing transaction costs involved in marketing farm produce. The head of ITC's agribusiness reports that the company's procurement costs have fallen since e-Choupal was implemented. And that's despite paying higher prices to its farmers: The program has enabled the company to eliminate multiple transportation, bagging, and handling steps—from farm to local market, from market to broker, from broker to processor—that did not add value in the chain.

INNOVATION

BOP markets are hotbeds of commercial and technological experimentation. The Swedish wireless company Ericsson, for instance, has developed a small cellular

telephone system, called a MiniGSM, that local operators
in BOP markets can use to offer cell phone service to a
small area at a radically lower cost than conventional
equipment entails. Packaged for easy shipment and
deployment, it provides stand-alone or networked voice
and data communications for up to 5,000 users within a
35-kilometer radius. Capital costs to the operator can be
as low as $4 per user, assuming a shared-use model with
individual phones operated by local entrepreneurs. The
MIT Media Lab, in collaboration with the Indian government, is developing low-cost devices that allow people to
use voice commands to communicate—without key-
boards—with various Internet sites in multiple languages. These new access devices promise to be far less
complex than traditional computers but would perform
many of the same basic functions.[2]

As we have seen, connectivity is a big issue for BOP
consumers. Companies that can find ways to dramatically lower connection costs, therefore, will have a very
strong market position. And that is exactly what the
Indian company n-Logue is trying to do. It connects hundreds of franchised village kiosks containing both a computer and a phone with centralized nodes that are, in
turn, connected to the national phone network and the
Internet. Each node, also a franchise, can serve between
30,000 and 50,000 customers, providing phone, e-mail,
Internet services, and relevant local information at
affordable prices to villagers in rural India. Capital costs
for the n-Logue system are now about $400 per wireless
"line" and are projected to decline to $100—at least ten
times lower than conventional telecom costs. On a per-
customer basis, the cost may amount to as little as $1.[3]
This appears to be a powerful model for ending rural iso-
lation and linking untapped rural markets to the global
economy.

New wireless technologies are likely to spur further business model innovations and lower costs even more. Ultrawideband, for example, is currently licensed in the United States only for limited, very low-power applications, in part because it spreads a signal across already-crowded portions of the broadcast spectrum. In many developing countries, however, the spectrum is less congested. In fact, the U.S.-based Dandin Group is already building an ultrawideband communications system for the Kingdom of Tonga, whose population of about 100,000 is spread over dozens of islands, making it a test bed for a next-generation technology that could transform the economics of Internet access.

E-commerce systems that run over the phone or the Internet are enormously important in BOP markets because they eliminate the need for layers of intermediaries. Consider how the U.S. start-up Voxiva has changed the way information is shared and business is transacted in Peru. The company partners with Telefónica, the dominant local carrier, to offer automated business applications over the phone. The inexpensive services include voice mail, data entry, and order placement; customers can check account balances, monitor delivery status, and access prerecorded information directories. According to the Boston Consulting Group, the Peruvian Ministry of Health uses Voxiva to disseminate information, take pharmaceutical orders, and link health care workers spread across 6,000 offices and clinics. Microfinance institutions use Voxiva to process loan applications and communicate with borrowers. Voxiva offers Web-based services, too, but far more of its potential customers in Latin America have access to a phone.

E-commerce companies are not the only ones turning the limitations of BOP markets to strategic advantage. A lack of dependable electric power stimulated the

UK-based start-up Freeplay Group to introduce hand-cranked radios in South Africa that subsequently became popular with hikers in the United States. Similar breakthroughs are being pioneered in the use of solar-powered devices such as battery chargers and water pumps. In China, where pesticide costs have often limited the use of modern agricultural techniques, there are now 13,000 small farmers—more than in the rest of the world combined—growing cotton that has been genetically engineered to be pest resistant.

Strategies for Serving BOP Markets

Certainly, succeeding in BOP markets requires multinationals to think creatively. The biggest change, though, has to come in the attitudes and practices of executives. Unless CEOs and other business leaders confront their own preconceptions, companies are unlikely to master the challenges of BOP markets. The traditional workforce is so rigidly conditioned to operate in higher-margin markets that, without formal training, it is unlikely to see the vast potential of the BOP market. The most pressing need, then, is education. Perhaps MNCs should create the equivalent of the Peace Corps: Having young managers spend a couple of formative years in BOP markets would open their eyes to the promise and the realities of doing business there.

To date, few multinationals have developed a cadre of people who are comfortable with these markets. Hindustan Lever is one of the exceptions. The company expects executive recruits to spend at least eight weeks in the villages of India to get a gut-level experience of Indian BOP markets. The new executives must become involved in some community project—building a road, cleaning up a water catchment area, teaching in a school, improving a health clinic. The goal is to engage with the local population. To buttress this effort, Hindustan Lever is initiating a massive program for managers at all levels—from the CEO down—to reconnect with their poorest customers. They'll talk with the poor in both rural and urban areas, visit the shops these customers frequent, and ask them about their experience with the company's products and those of its competitors.

In addition to expanding managers' understanding of BOP markets, companies will need to make structural changes. To capitalize on the innovation potential of these markets, for example, they might set up R&D units in developing countries that are specifically focused on local opportunities. When Hewlett-Packard launched its e-Inclusion division, which concentrates on rural markets, it established a branch of its famed HP Labs in India charged with developing products and services explicitly for this market. Hindustan Lever maintains a significant R&D effort in India, as well.

Companies might also create venture groups and internal investment funds aimed at seeding entrepreneurial efforts in BOP markets. Such investments reap direct benefits in terms of business experience and market development. They can also play an indirect but vital role in growing the overall BOP market in sectors that will ultimately benefit the multinational. At least one major U.S. corporation is planning to launch such a fund, and the G8's Digital Opportunity Task Force is proposing a similar one focused on digital ventures.

MNCs should also consider creating a business development task force aimed at these markets. Assembling a diverse group of people from across the corporation and empowering it to function as a skunk works team that ignores conventional dogma will likely lead to greater innovation. Companies that have tried this approach have been surprised by the amount of interest such a task force generates. Many employees want to work on projects that have the potential to make a real difference in improving the lives of the poor. When Hewlett-Packard announced its e-Inclusion division, for example, it was overwhelmed by far more volunteers than it could accommodate.

Making internal changes is important, but so is reaching out to external partners. Joining with businesses that are already established in these markets can be an effective entry strategy, since these companies will naturally understand the market dynamics better. In addition to limiting the risks for each player, partnerships also maximize the existing infrastructure—both physical and social. MNCs seeking partners should look beyond businesses to NGOs and community groups. They are key sources of knowledge about customers' behavior, and they often experiment the most with new services and new delivery models. In fact, of the social enterprises experimenting with creative uses of digital technology that the Digital Dividend Project Clearinghouse tracked, nearly 80% are NGOs. In Namibia, for instance, an organization called SchoolNet is providing low-cost, alternative technology solutions—such as solar power and wireless approaches—to schools and community-based groups throughout the country. SchoolNet is currently linking as many as 35 new schools every month.

Entrepreneurs also will be critical partners. According to an analysis by McKinsey & Company, the rapid growth of cable TV in India—there are 50 million connections a decade after introduction—is largely due to small entrepreneurs. These individuals have been building the last mile of the network, typically by putting a satellite dish on their own houses and laying cable to connect their neighbors. A note of caution, however. Entrepreneurs in BOP markets lack access to the advice, technical help, seed funding, and business support services available in the industrial world. So MNCs may need to take on mentoring roles or partner with local business development organizations that can help entrepreneurs create investment and partnering opportunities.

It's worth noting that, contrary to popular opinion, women play a significant role in the economic development of these regions. MNCs, therefore, should pay particular attention to women entrepreneurs. Women are also likely to play the most critical role in product acceptance not only because of their childcare and household management activities but also because of the social capital that they have built up in their communities. Listening to and educating such customers is essential for success.

Regardless of the opportunities, many companies will consider the bottom of the pyramid to be too risky. We've shown how partnerships can limit risk; another option is to enter into consortia. Imagine sharing the costs of building a rural network with the communications company that would operate it, a consumer goods company seeking channels to expand its sales, and a bank that is financing the construction and wants to make loans to and collect deposits from rural customers.

Investing where powerful synergies exist will also mitigate risk. The Global Digital Opportunity Initiative, a partnership of the Markle Foundation and the UN Development Programme, will help a small number of countries implement a strategy to harness the power of information and communications technologies to increase development. The countries will be chosen in part based on their interest and their willingness to make supportive regulatory and market reforms. To concentrate resources and create reinforcing effects, the initiative will encourage international aid agencies and global companies to assist with implementation.

All of the strategies we've outlined here will be of little use, however, unless the external barriers we've touched on—poor infrastructure, inadequate connectivity, corrupt intermediaries, and the like—are removed. Here's where technology holds the most promise. Information and communications technologies can grant access to otherwise isolated communities, provide marketing and distribution channels, bypass intermediaries, drive down transaction costs, and help aggregate demand and buying power. Smart cards and other emerging technologies are inexpensive ways to give poor customers a secure identity, a transaction or credit history, and even a virtual address—prerequisites for interacting with the formal economy. That's why high-tech companies aren't the only ones that should be interested in closing the global digital divide; encouraging the spread of low-cost digital networks at the bottom of the pyramid is a priority for virtually all companies that want to enter and engage with these markets. Improved connectivity is an important catalyst for more effective markets, which are critical to boosting income levels and accelerating economic growth. (See "Sharing Intelligence" at the end of this article.)

Moreover, global companies stand to gain from the effects of network expansion in these markets. According to Metcalfe's Law, the usefulness of a network equals the square of the number of users. By the same logic, the value and vigor of the economic activity that will be generated when hundreds of thousands of previously isolated rural communities can buy and sell from one another and from urban markets will increase dramatically—to the benefit of all participants.

Since bop markets require significant rethinking of managerial practices, it is legitimate for managers to ask: Is it worth the effort?

We think the answer is yes. For one thing, big corporations should solve big problems—and what is a more pressing concern than alleviating the poverty that 4 billion people are currently mired in? It is hard to argue that the wealth of technology and talent within leading multinationals is better allocated to producing incremental variations of existing products than to addressing the real needs—and real opportunities—at the bottom of the pyramid. Moreover, through competition, multinationals are likely to bring to BOP markets a level of accountability for performance and resources that neither international development agencies nor national governments have demonstrated during the last 50 years. Participation by MNCs could set a new standard, as well as a new market-driven paradigm, for addressing poverty.

But ethical concerns aside, we've shown that the potential for expanding the bottom of the market is just too great to ignore. Big companies need to focus on big market opportunities if they want to generate real growth. It is simply good business strategy to be involved in large, untapped markets that offer new customers, cost-saving opportunities, and access to radical innovation. The business opportunities at the bottom of the pyramid are real, and they are open to any MNC willing to engage and learn.

Sharing Intelligence

WHAT CREATIVE NEW APPROACHES to serving the bottom-of-the-pyramid markets have digital technologies made possible? Which sectors or countries show the most economic activity or the fastest growth? What new business models show promise? What kinds of partnerships—for funding, distribution, public relations—have been most successful?

The Digital Dividend Project Clearinghouse (digitaldividend.org) helps answer those types of questions. The Web site tracks the activities of organizations that use digital tools to provide connectivity and deliver services to underserved populations in developing countries. Currently, it contains information on 700 active projects around the world. Maintained under the auspices of the nonprofit World Resources Institute, the site lets participants in different projects share experiences and swap knowledge with one another. Moreover, the site provides data for trend analyses and other specialized studies that facilitate market analyses, local partnerships, and rapid, low-cost learning.

Notes

1. Andrew Lawlor, Caitlin Peterson, and Vivek Sandell, "Catalyzing Rural Development: TARAhaat.com" (World Resources Institute, July 2001).

2. Michael Best and Colin M. Maclay, "Community Internet Access in Rural Areas: Solving the Economic Sustainability

Puzzle," *The Global Information Technology Report 2001–2002: Readiness for the Networked World,* ed., Geoffrey Kirkman (Oxford University Press, 2002), available online at http://www.cid.harvard.edu/cr/gitrr_030202.html.

3. Joy Howard, Erik Simanis, and Charis Simms, "Sustainable Deployment for Rural Connectivity: The n-Logue Model" (World Resources Institute, July 2001).

Originally published in September 2002
Reprint R0209C

The Battle for China's Good-Enough Market

ORIT GADIESH, PHILIP LEUNG,
AND TILL VESTRING

Executive Summary

A CRITICAL NEW BATTLEGROUND is emerging in
China: It's the "good-enough" market segment—home of
reliable enough products at low-enough prices to attract
the cream of the country's fast-growing cohort of midlevel
consumers.

Traditionally, foreign multinationals have dominated
China's premium segment, while a plethora of domestic
companies have served the low end, often unprofitably.
But as middle-class buying power increases, and the tolerance for high markups at the top end wanes, the middle market is growing quickly.

Thriving in a market so big is clearly important in itself.
But, argue Bain chairman Gadiesh and Bain partners
Leung and Vestring, competition in this particular arena
has more far-reaching implications. Companies that flour-
ish in China's middle market today are learning valuable
lessons they need to compete worldwide: Multinationals

are discovering how to focus products downscale to break out of the premium tier, and domestic firms are building scale and marketing expertise to move up. Both are positioning themselves to export their China offerings to other large emerging markets such as India and Brazil—and, after that, to the developed markets. Ultimately, the authors warn, the good-enough space, where multinationals and Chinese firms are going head-to-head, is the one from which the world's leading companies will emerge.

The authors describe three strategies for entering and prevailing in this strategically vital space. Multinationals can attack domestic players from above, Chinese firms operating in the low end can burrow up from below, and both can acquire their way into it. The experiences of such players as Colgate-Palmolive, GM, GE, Huawei Technologies, Haier, and Ningbo Bird show how challenging it is to gain a foothold in the middle market but also how much potential there is to use it as a springboard for global expansion.

CATERPILLAR, the world leader in construction equipment, is having trouble making deeper tracks in China. The U.S.-based manufacturer of tractors, backhoes, road graders, and other devices began selling equipment in China in 1975, a year before the death of Chairman Mao. As the Chinese government invested massively in infrastructure, Caterpillar helped pave the way, literally, for economic growth and modernization in the world's fastest-growing market for construction equipment.

Like many foreign players in any number of industries, Caterpillar got its start in China by selling goods to the Chinese government—the only possible customer before the era of economic reform—and then began selling high-quality equipment to the private sector as a premium segment of the market emerged. But it never broadened its focus to include other segments, and by the early 2000s, Komatsu, Hitachi, Daewoo, and other competitors from Japan and Korea were in the middle market with tools and equipment that cost less but were still reliable. Meanwhile, a tranche of local manufacturers that had previously been focused only on the low end of the market were burrowing up to battle the established players, designing and releasing their own products targeted squarely at middle-market consumers.

As the experiences of Caterpillar and other multinationals suggest, a critical new battleground is emerging for companies seeking to establish, sustain, or expand their presence in China: It's the "good-enough" market segment, home of reliable-enough products at low-enough prices to attract the cream of China's fast-growing cohort of midlevel consumers.

Harvard professor Clay Christensen, author of *The Innovator's Dilemma*, has used the phrase "good enough" to suggest that start-up companies developing and releasing new products and services don't necessarily need to aim for perfection to make inroads against established players. The phrase can be similarly applied to middle-market players in China that have been able to steal a march on incumbents by developing and releasing good-enough products that are displacing premium ones.

These forward-thinking companies (multinational and domestic firms alike) are doing more than just seizing share of wallet and share of mind in China's rapidly expanding middle market—in and of itself a major achievement. They are conditioning themselves for worldwide competition tomorrow: They're building the scale, expertise, and business capabilities they'll need to export their China offerings to other large emerging markets (India and Brazil, for instance) and, ultimately, to the developed markets. Given China's share of global market growth (Goldman Sachs estimates that China will account for 36% of the world's incremental GDP between 2000 and 2030) and the country's role in preparing companies to pursue opportunities in other developing regions, it's becoming clear that businesses wanting to succeed globally will need to win in China first.

In the following pages, we'll explore the importance of China as a lead market. We'll describe the surge of activity in China's middle market; when (and whether) multinationals and Chinese companies should enter this vibrant arena for growth; and, most important, how they can compete effectively in the good-enough segment. As Caterpillar and other foreign players have learned, achieving leadership in China's middle market isn't easy.

An Evolving Opportunity

Historically, there has been a simple structure to China's markets: at the top, a small premium segment served by foreign companies realizing solid margins and rapid growth; at the bottom, a large low-end segment served by local companies offering low-quality, undifferentiated products (typically 40% to 90% cheaper than premium ones) that often lose money—when producers do their accounting right. Between the two is the rapidly expanding good-enough segment. (For an example of how one market sector breaks out, see the exhibit "The Structure of China's Market for Televisions.")

The good-enough space in China is growing for many reasons, not the least of which are recent shifts in consumer buying patterns and preferences. These shifts are coming from two directions: Consumers with rising incomes are trading up from the low-end products they previously purchased. At the same time, higher-income consumers are moving away from pricey foreign brands and accepting less expensive, locally produced alternatives of reasonable quality. The same holds true on the B2B front.

Consequently, China's middle market is growing faster than both the premium and low-end segments. In some

The Structure of China's Market for Televisions

Premium (Narrow)	Good-Enough (Rapidly Expanding)	Low-End (Evolving Base)
Definition: High-end products purchased by discerning customers with significant purchasing power.	Definition: Products of good quality, produced by local companies for a rapidly expanding group of value-seeking consumers with midlevel incomes.	Definition: Products of lower quality, meeting basic needs, produced by local firms for a large group of consumers with low incomes.
Leading vendors: Panasonic, Philips, Sony	Leading vendors: Hisense, Skyworth, TCL	Leading vendor: Konka
Product features: LCD and plasma screens, many state-of-the-art user features, priced according to their status as international brands.	Product features: LCD, plasma, and large cathode-ray tube screens, with limited user features, priced to undercut foreign brands.	Product features: Cathode-ray tube screens with basic standard user features and low-cost components, priced to sell.
Share of market in 2005: 13%	Share of market in 2005: 62%	Share of market in 2005: 25%

categories, the good-enough space already accounts for nearly half of all revenues. Eight out of every ten washing machines and televisions now sold in China are good-enough brands. It should come as no surprise, then, that China—and, in particular, its opportunity-rich middle market—is increasingly capturing multinational executives' resources and attention. As Mark Bernhard, chief financial officer of General Motors' Shanghai-based GM China Group, recently told the Detroit News: "For GM to remain a global industry leader, we must also be a leader in China."

The automaker's strategy in China embodies that belief. GM had traditionally been an underperformer in the market for small cars. However, its acquisition of Korea's ailing Daewoo Motor in 2002 enabled it to compete and ultimately take a leadership position in China. The deal allowed GM to develop new models for half what it would cost the company to develop them in the West. Daewoo-designed cars now make up more than 50% of GM's sales in China, currently its second biggest market. What's more, GM is using these vehicles to compete against Asian automakers and sell small cars in more than 150 markets around the world, from India to the United States.

Colgate-Palmolive made similar moves in China. It entered into a joint venture in the early 1990s with one of China's largest toothpaste producers, and it acquired China's market leader for toothbrushes a decade later, allowing it to scale up and then leverage its production processes to compete in other parts of the world. As a result, Colgate more than doubled its oral hygiene revenues in China between 1998 and 2005, and it now exports its China products to 70 countries.

Local Chinese competitors pose the biggest challenge to multinationals seeking to capitalize on their business ventures in China and beyond. In the auto industry, for instance, domestic carmakers like Geely and Chery have eaten away at Western companies' market share in China by introducing good-enough cars for local consumption. Several of these automakers have started exhibiting vehicles at car shows in the United States and Europe, buying available Western brands, and exporting vehicles to other emerging markets. True, these players face enormous challenges in meeting safety and emissions standards and in building up the required distribution networks to compete in Europe and North America. But no Western company should underestimate the determination of Chinese firms to figure out how to meet international quality standards and make their global mark.

European and North American companies producing major appliances, microwaves, and televisions know this all too well. They abdicated China to low-cost local competitors in the 1990s and now find themselves struggling to compete globally against those same Chinese companies. Haier, which started making refrigerators in 1984, went on to become one of China's best-known brands and then used its hard-won scale advantages and manufacturing skills to crack, and then dominate, foreign markets. Today, it is one of the largest refrigerator companies in the world, controlling 8.3% of the highly fragmented global market. The company sells products in more than 100 markets, including the United States, Africa, and Pakistan.

Obviously, the stakes in China have changed. Local companies are using booming domestic markets to hone their strategies at home before taking on the world. Multinationals, therefore, need to defend their positions in China not only to profit from the economic growth in that country but also to prevent local competitors from becoming global threats. The good-enough space is where multinationals and Chinese firms are going head-to-head—and it's the market segment from which the world's leading companies will emerge.

Making an Entrance

It's one thing to recognize the importance of China's middle market; it's another thing entirely to turn that awareness into action. The first step in winning the battle for China's good-enough market is determining when—or when not—to enter the fray. That will depend on the attractiveness of the premium segment: Is it still growing? Are companies still achieving high returns or are returns eroding? Another consideration is your company's market position: Are you a leader or a niche player? (See the exhibit "Should You Enter the Middle Market?")

Foreign companies grappling with the good-enough decision in China will need to consider these factors and perform thorough market and competitor analyses, along with careful customer segmentation and needs analyses—classic strategy tools, of course, but applied in the context of a rapidly changing economy that may lack historical data on market share, prices, and the like. Senior managers will need to establish the factors that are key to success in everything from branding to pricing to distribution. This knowledge will inform important decisions about whether companies should expand organically into the middle market, acquire an existing player in that space, or find a good-enough partner.

Generally speaking, competing in the good-enough space is neither necessary nor wise for multinationals operating in stable premium segments. These companies should instead focus on lowering their costs and innovating to maintain their premium or niche positions and to sustain their margins. We studied one large manufacturer of automation equipment, for example, that wisely decided to stand pat in the premium segment. Market research suggested that its customers were still willing to pay more for reliability, even with a variety of lower-cost choices out there. The company continued to invest in R&D, hoping to further differentiate its products from

Should You Enter the Middle Market?

Multinationals deciding whether to move into China's middle market need to first consider the attractiveness of the premium segment and their current market position. If conditions warrant, they can attack aggressively from above. Chinese firms can burrow up from below. Both can acquire their way into the good-enough space.

State of the Premium Market Segment

	Strong	Weak or eroding
Companies' Competitive Position — Strong	**Maintain strong premium status** Hold off on entering the good-enough segment of the market—for now. Drop prices as required to remain competitive; lower costs and innovate to defend premium status and sustain margin. Regularly reevaluate the decision not to enter.	**Attack from above or buy your way in** Premium players employ an offensive-defense approach to enter the middle market. That is, they enter the good-enough segment in order to defend against the erosion of the premium segment.
Companies' Competitive Position — Weak or eroding	**Innovate to maintain current premium status** Hold off on entering the good-enough segment of the market—for now. Increase innovation efforts to capture a niche position in the premium segment. Regularly reevaluate the decision not to enter.	**Burrow up from below or buy your way in** Value players enter the good-enough segment using a breakthrough approach—with a merger, for instance, or by developing China-specific products or business models—to steal share from incumbents and attain market leadership.

those of local players; it expanded its distribution and service networks to improve its responsiveness to customers; and it cut costs by taking advantage of local production resources.

Few multinationals find themselves in such a fortunate position, however. If growth in the premium segment is slowing and returns are eroding, multinational corporations will need to enter the good-enough space. Even those companies that because of their strong competitive position initially abstain from entering the middle market should revisit their decision frequently to guard against emerging competitive threats. For their part, Chinese companies will need to move upmarket as the lower-end segment becomes increasingly competitive.

Our research and experience indicate that companies contemplating a move into the good-enough space go about it in one of three basic ways: Leading multinationals in the premium segment *attack from above.* The goal for these organizations is to lower their manufacturing costs, introduce simplified products or services, and broaden their distribution networks while maintaining reasonable quality. Meanwhile, Chinese challengers in the low-end segment tend to *burrow up from below.* These companies aim to take the legs out from under established players by providing new offerings that ratchet up quality but cost consumers much less than the premium products do. And, finally, multinationals that can't reduce their costs fast enough, and domestic players looking for more skills, technology, and talent, *buy their way in.*

Each of these moves comes with its own set of traps. The challenge, then, for companies eyeing the middle market is to understand why those that went before them failed in this space—and how to sidestep the pitfalls they encountered. Let's take a closer look at these three approaches.

Attacking from Above

Whether they're selling toothpaste or power transmission equipment, multinational companies dominate China's small but high-margin premium segment—the only one in which foreign players have traditionally been able to compete successfully. So a move toward the middle certainly holds a fair amount of risk for those already thriving in the premium space. A chief concern is cannibalization. After all, selling to consumers in less-than-premium segments could negatively affect sales of high-end products. These companies also run the risk of fueling gray markets for their wares. If, say, a business sells a T-shirt for $10 in China but $20 in the United States, there's a good chance an enterprising distributor will find a way to buy that T-shirt in China and export it to the United States for sale there.

Multinational managers, therefore, need to conduct careful market analyses to understand the differences between China's premium and good-enough segments. There may be, for instance, strong geographic distinctions a company can capitalize on. Consider the strategy GE Healthcare employed to expand sales of its MRI equipment in China. The company created a line of simplified machines targeted at hospitals in China's remote and financially constrained second- and third-tier cities—places like Hefei and Lanzhou, where other multinationals rarely ventured. That good-enough territory had all the right conditions: It was a fast-growing market whose customers' purchasing criteria weren't likely to change soon. GE's cost structure allowed it to

compete with other middle-market players in the industry. And there was little risk that the company would
cannibalize its premium line of diagnostic machines;
large city hospitals were not keen on downgrading their
MRI equipment.

Markets are dynamic, and there's no place on the
planet where they are shifting as quickly or as dramatically as in China. So multinational executives also need
to think about the degree to which the premium and
good-enough segments will converge over time. Managers can use traditional forecasting methods (scenario
planning, war gaming, consultations with leading-edge
customers, and so on) to pick up on emerging threats
and impending opportunities. Which brings us back to
GE Healthcare's MRI expansion plans: The company's
long-held commitment to health care development in
China meshed perfectly with Chinese leaders' publicly
stated desire to improve health services in less-privileged
areas of the country. Given the government's aims, GE
Healthcare understood there would eventually be some
overlap of the premium, middle, and low-end markets—
and profitable opportunities in the good-enough space.

After weighing the risks that cannibalization and
dynamic markets pose to their company's premium positioning, managers in multinationals need to consider
their possible opportunities in the good-enough space:
Can they take advantage of their lower purchasing costs,
greater manufacturing scale, and distribution synergies?
Then they have to determine which capabilities they may
need to develop: How adept is their organization at
designing products, services, brands, and sales
approaches that will attract customers in the middle
market without diminishing their company's position in
the premium space? They may need to convene teams

dedicated solely to studying the opportunities and resources required in the good-enough segment, as GE Healthcare did. (See "Penetrating the Good-Enough Market, One County Hospital at a Time" at the end of this article.) They may also want to recruit local management talent—individuals with experience competing in the middle space—or purchase local companies to gain new technologies or expertise.

Those multinationals that decide to enter the middle market tend to employ an "offensive-defense" strategy—aggressively staking claims in the good-enough space to box out emerging local players and established global competitors seeking to gain their own scale advantages. By entering the good-enough space ahead of the pack, for instance, GE Healthcare was able to defend its position against local upstarts, including Mindray, Wandong, and Anke. The company is still trying to develop the optimal product portfolio and is addressing such issues as how best to service the equipment. Even so, GE captured 52% of the $238 million market in 2004, generating roughly $120 million in sales. Having honed its approach to the good-enough space, GE is replicating the strategy in new markets in several developing countries, including India.

Multinationals are bound to find it tough to jump in from above. Apart from the risks of cannibalization and all the challenges always associated with going down-market, companies will need to adapt fast, as customers' preferences change and competitors react. And they will probably need to tear apart the cost structure of their good-enough competitors to understand how those firms make money while charging such low prices. Just switching to local sourcing, for instance, may not be sufficient for large multinationals to match the lower production costs of their domestic competitors.

Burrowing Up from Below

Multinationals for years underestimated the ability and desire of local players in the low end of the market to move up and compete—a miscalculation that may now be coming home to roost. Recent developments have strengthened local competition in China and facilitated Chinese companies' moves upmarket and beyond.

Let's start with consolidation. For years, there were often hundreds of companies in a single industry catering primarily to customers in the low end of the market and typically focusing on regional needs. Many of those companies operated unprofitably—think of Red Star Appliances or Wuhan Xi Dao Industrial Stock. Because of China's free-market reforms, however, the weakest of those competitors are folding, and industries are experiencing waves of consolidation. Red Star, Wuhan Xi Dao, and 16 other money-losing concerns shifted and reshifted throughout the 1990s to form appliance maker Haier. A competent player or two, like Haier, have risen in each industry, often benefiting from national support. China's booming economy has enabled these survivors to build scale and develop market capabilities such as R&D and branding. As we have seen, over time, several of these emerging domestic champions have become direct challengers to global companies in a variety of industries.

Next, look at the rapidly expanding customer base in the middle space. Chinese customers—whether individual consumers, businesses, or government agencies—are becoming less willing to shell out 70% to 100% premiums for international products. At most, they may pay 20% to 30% more for world-class brands. The Italian dairy giant Parmalat discovered exactly that when it tried selling fruit-flavored yogurt for the equivalent of 24 cents a cup.

Instead, consumers went with local brands at half the price. It seemed that brand, innovation, and quality—the hallmarks of multinationals in China—were no longer critical points of differentiation in customers' minds. This price sensitivity is opening up new ground for ambitious Chinese companies traditionally focused on the low end. These firms are designing and releasing good-enough products that overcome buyers' skepticism about quality at much lower prices, which generate higher margins than their low-end products. The often brutal competitive dynamics in the low-end segment also serve as a huge incentive for the better-managed local companies to move up. Until consumer demand began to explode in China, however, there really wasn't anywhere for these firms to go. Now there is.

The journey from low end to good-enough to global usually takes a decade and then some—but more and more Chinese companies are embarking on it. For instance, Lenovo, founded in 1984, entered the good-enough segment via a joint venture, flourished in the middle market, and then went on to establish its international brand with the purchase of IBM's PC division in 2005 for $1.75 billion. It is currently the world's third-largest PC maker. Similarly, Huawei Technologies has grown since 1988 to the point where 31 of the first 50 firms on Standard & Poor's ranking of the world's top telecom companies are clients of the Chinese maker of mobile and fixed telecommunications networks.

Just as foreign players approaching the market from above come face-to-face with their shortcomings—high costs, limited distribution capabilities, and the possibility of cannibalizing their own products—local companies moving up encounter their own limitations. Foremost is the shortage of managerial talent, especially for international businesses. Growing numbers of Chinese students are pursuing MBAs and studying abroad. They are slowly distinguishing themselves from the large cohort of current Chinese managers, whose command-and-control leadership style dominates local manufacturing houses. But catching up remains difficult, as China's surging economic growth outpaces the country's ability to educate and apprentice twenty-first-century managers.

Another obstacle for Chinese companies is their inability to compete with global players through innovation or by establishing a strong brand because of their limited size and their lack of management tools and experience. A question like "How much should we spend on advertising?" can stymie local managers looking at expansion. Long used to competing solely on price, they have little experience in understanding and addressing segment-specific needs, linking those needs to R&D and brand-building efforts, and creating the required infrastructure in sales and distribution.

Consider the early successes enjoyed by Chinese handset manufacturer Ningbo Bird. It was among a group of small, local companies that took 20% to 30% of the telecom market between 2000 and 2002 from the likes of Nokia and Motorola. Ningbo Bird prevailed by competing on price. But its success was short-lived, its march toward global expansion thwarted. The company just didn't have the expertise and resources the foreign corporations had in customer segmentation, R&D, innovation, and distribution.

By contrast, Huawei has been able to successfully navigate such roadblocks. Initially established as a network equipment distributor, Huawei has built and acquired the technical and managerial capabilities it needed to rise up from the low end of the market. From its inception, Huawei invested 10% of its sales in R&D. It developed its own products to penetrate new segments in China and forged technical alliances to further broaden its product mix. With government support, Huawei prompted consolidation in the domestic market, gaining massive scale in the process. The company now controls 14% of the local market for telecom networks. Firmly established in the good-enough space at home, Huawei built brands to meet the requirements of global customers. It established 12 R&D centers around the world, pioneering next-generation technologies (customized communication networks and voice access systems) and partnering with global brands such as 3Com to build customer awareness of its own brands.

Huawei has broadened its reach in stages over 14 years. The company first focused on establishing itself in developing regions of China, where multinationals had less incentive to compete. It then penetrated countries with emerging economies, such as Russia and Brazil. Finally, it attacked the developed countries. It has expanded internationally through aggressive sales and marketing, by taking advantage of low-cost China-based R&D, and by leveraging its ability to outsource some of its manufacturing processes to other players in China. A little more than a decade ago, Huawei was a regional company in a local market that few multinationals considered important. With 2005 revenues of $8.2 billion, it is now second only to Cisco, according to InfoTech Trends' ranking of the networking hardware industry. It could never have ascended the way it has without using China's good-enough segment as a springboard for growth.

Buying Your Way In

For multinational companies that can't alter their costs or processes quickly enough to compete with local players, and for Chinese firms that lack the production scale, R&D mechanisms, and customer-facing capabilities to compete with foreign players, there is still a breakthrough option for entering the middle market—mergers and acquisitions.

China's entry into the World Trade Organization in 2001 fueled a surge in M&A activity. Now, however, foreign acquirers are facing tougher approval processes. China's public commitment to open markets remains strong, but several high-profile deals have gotten stuck at the provincial or ministerial level, owing to increasing public concerns about selling out to foreign firms. For instance, in its bid to buy Xugong Group Construction Machinery, China's largest construction machinery manufacturer and distributor, the U.S. private equity firm Carlyle Group met with unexpected resistance from the government and ended up twice reducing its stake, ultimately to 45%. In rejecting successive Carlyle bids, officials in Beijing insisted the nation's construction equipment industry should be controlled by "domestic hands."

As the Carlyle Group learned, gaining regulatory and political approval for M&As in China is a major undertaking. Foreign companies seeking such approval may need to draft (and redraft) a compelling business case for the acquisition, one that cites up front the benefits for local companies and authorities. Like Carlyle, they must be willing to adjust (and readjust) the structure, terms, and conditions of a deal to gain government support. They may also need to engage in heavy-duty relationship building, investing the time and resources required to woo critical players in the deal.

As is always the case with M&As the world over, it's all about fit: There should be cost and distribution synergies between the multinational and its target and little chance that the local company's products will cannibalize the multinational's premium brands. Successful acquirers in China—multinationals and Chinese firms alike—use a clear strategic rationale to select the right target. They overinvest in the due diligence process. They take a systematic approach to postmerger integration.

That was the game plan behind Gillette's 2003 acquisition of Nanfu, then China's leading battery manufacturer. Gillette's Duracell division throughout the 1990s was losing market share in China to lower-priced competitors. By 2002, Duracell's share of the Chinese domestic battery market was 6.5%. By contrast, Nanfu controlled more than half the market. After careful analysis, Gillette's management team recognized that its Duracell unit was at a cost disadvantage compared with its rivals and concluded it would be difficult to broaden the brand's market penetration. Facing such odds, Gillette decided to buy into the good-enough market, acquiring a majority stake in Nanfu. But Gillette was extremely careful to protect both Duracell's and Nanfu's brands in their respective segments. Gillette continues to sell premium batteries in China under the Duracell brand and has maintained Nanfu as the leading national brand for the mass market. The dual branding, cost synergies, sales growth, broadened product portfolio, economies of scale, and distribution to more than 3 million retail outlets in China have paid off for Gillette, which has seen significant increases in its operating margins in China.

Buying into the good-enough segment also worked for consumer-goods giants Danone, L'Oréal, and Anheuser-Busch—companies that saw the vast potential in China but couldn't get their costs low enough to compete. For instance, in 2004, Anheuser-Busch outbid its competitor SABMiller to acquire Harbin, the fourth-largest brewer in China. That acquisition allowed Anheuser-Busch to reach the masses while preventing Harbin from swimming upstream. The next year, it increased its stake in Tsingtao Brewery, from 9.9% to 27%. Both moves enabled the global brewer to rapidly increase its share among China's drinkers of less-than-premium beer.

Chinese companies are also wrapping their arms around acquisition strategies, attempting to establish their presence in the middle market by purchasing brands, talent, and other resources from target companies in Europe and North America. To date, they've met with mixed results. On the one hand, Lenovo's acquisition of IBM's PC division turned the Chinese computer maker into the world's third-largest PC company. On the other hand, the acquisition experiences of TCL, a major Chinese consumer electronics manufacturer, have been less successful.

TCL built a strong position in the Chinese market by producing and distributing basic cathode-ray tube TVs at astonishingly low prices. It also engaged in contract and private-label manufacturing for the U.S. and European markets. But TCL realized it would need a strong brand to rise up from the low end of the China market and that growing organically in a mature industry like TV manufacturing would be prohibitively expensive. So TCL acquired French firm Thomson, which owned a number of well-known brands, including RCA. Unfortunately, Thomson also owned some high-cost and unproductive manufacturing facilities in France. TCL has struggled since acquiring Thomson, as the market for TVs has shifted from cathode-ray to plasma and LCD technologies. In 2006, the company lost $351 million from operations. Many Chinese companies believe that in order to play in the global arena, they must simply forge ahead, buying established Western brands and distribution systems—whether or not they have the experience and management tools to handle such acquisitions. But, as TCL's story suggests, executing such a plan is hardly cut-and-dried.

IN THE 1960S AND 1970S, the mantra for many organizations was "Capture U.S. market share, capture the world." Today, China—and its middle market in particular—has become the object of multinationals' ardent pursuit. The enormous market potential of the country's population, the formidable growth of the economy, and China's established position in low-cost sourcing and manufacturing are providing competitive advantages for many companies—benefits these organizations are then leveraging both inside and outside the nation.

Local Chinese companies know their futures depend on entering the good-enough space and attacking global leaders (and their premium positioning) by offering low-cost products of reasonable quality that they can eventually take to the world. Multinationals are beginning to recognize that ceding the middle space to Chinese firms may breed competitors that will ultimately challenge them on a global scale. Ironically, Chinese companies that have already gone global are on the defensive as well. A recent *Forbes Asia* article reported that as Haier has attacked international markets and won share abroad, both local companies and multinationals have been nibbling away at its share of China's middle market—which fell from 29% in 2004 to 25% last year.

The stakes are high. All the more reason, then, for companies that have stumbled in China in the past to redouble their efforts. Danone's high product costs thwarted its early attempts to sell dairy products in China's middle market. But that obstacle was removed when the firm reengaged in the fight, lowering its costs by buying a local dairy.

Likewise, Caterpillar hasn't diverted its focus away from China and the importance of the good-enough space. The company plans to triple its sales by 2010, opening more manufacturing plants and dealerships and forming more joint ventures with local companies. "Operational and sales success in China is critical for the company's long-term growth and profitability," said Rich Lavin, vice president of Caterpillar's Asia Pacific Operations Division, in November 2006. Shortly thereafter, the company moved its divisional headquarters—from Tokyo to Beijing.

Penetrating the Good-Enough Market, One County Hospital at a Time

GE HEALTHCARE ALREADY HAD a successful business selling high-end medical equipment in China when the Chinese government set a goal for the next decade of improving the health care available in less-privileged locales. To support the government's efforts and also to break out of the high end of the market, GE developed a business case for manufacturing and selling medical devices for China's good-enough market. CEO Jeff Immelt's visits and conversations with Chinese leaders motivated the company to pursue the opportunity. In the end, GE's research and analysis identified a substantial demand from thousands of midtier and low-end Chinese hospitals in less affluent provinces that were not served by multinationals. GE knew that it could design new products and business models to serve this market. GE also knew that by using techniques like Six Sigma to eliminate manufacturing waste, it could make its costs competitive.

A team was charged with observing operations in the target hospitals and meeting with the hospital administrators and physicians to help determine what sort of medical equipment customers wanted, the specific features they needed, possible price points, and the kinds of distribution and services that would be required. Armed with this information, the fact-finding team considered stripping out some of the expensive equipment features and adding others that these target customers valued more. For instance, doctors in China's high-end hospitals preferred to program the medical equipment themselves, whereas physicians in the midlevel and low-end hospitals, who considered themselves less computer savvy, preferred preprogrammed machines.

The team worked with staffers in GE's R&D and manufacturing groups to build the right products at the right price points for the good-enough market. Because GE's existing sales, distribution, and service systems were not geared to the target customers, the company also had to reconfigure its networks of existing representatives and recruit new ones. This middle-market initiative is still a work in progress, but GE Healthcare has taken an enormous first step in establishing itself—and defending itself against rivals—in the good-enough segment.

Originally published in September 2007
Reprint R0709E

Strategies That Fit
Emerging Markets

TARUN KHANNA, KRISHNA G. PALEPU,
AND JAYANT SINHA

Executive Summary

IT'S NO EASY TASK to identify strategies for entering
new international markets or to decide which countries to
do business with. Many firms simply go with what they
know—and fall far short of their goals.

Part of the problem is that emerging markets have
"institutional voids": They lack specialized intermediaries,
regulatory systems, and contract-enforcing methods.
These gaps have made it difficult for multinationals to
succeed in developing nations; thus, many companies
have resisted investing there. That may be a mistake. If
Western companies don't come up with good strategies
for engaging with emerging markets, they are unlikely to
remain competitive.

Many firms choose their markets and strategies for
the wrong reasons, relying on everything from senior
managers' gut feelings to the behaviors of rivals. Corporations also depend on composite indexes for help

making decisions. But these analyses can be misleading; they don't account for vital information about the soft infrastructures in developing nations. A better approach is to understand institutional variations between countries. The best way to do this, the authors have found, is by using the five contexts framework.

The five contexts are a country's political and social systems, its degree of openness, its product markets, its labor markets, and its capital markets. By asking a series of questions that pertain to each of the five areas, executives can map the institutional contexts of any nation.

When companies match their strategies to each country's contexts, they can take advantage of a location's unique strengths. But first firms should weigh the benefits against the costs. If they find that the risks of adaptation are too great, they should try to change the contexts in which they operate or simply stay away.

CEOS AND TOP MANAGEMENT TEAMS of large corporations, particularly in North America, Europe, and Japan, acknowledge that globalization is the most critical challenge they face today. They are also keenly aware that it has become tougher during the past decade to identify internationalization strategies and to choose which countries to do business with. Still, most companies have stuck to the strategies they've traditionally deployed, which emphasize standardized approaches to new markets while sometimes experimenting with a few local twists. As a result, many multinational corporations are struggling to develop successful strategies in emerging markets.

Part of the problem, we believe, is that the absence of specialized intermediaries, regulatory systems, and

contract-enforcing mechanisms in emerging markets—
"institutional voids," we christened them in a 1997 HBR
article—hampers the implementation of globalization
strategies. Companies in developed countries usually
take for granted the critical role that "soft" infrastructure
plays in the execution of their business models in their
home markets. But that infrastructure is often underdeveloped or absent in emerging markets. There's no
dearth of examples. Companies can't find skilled market
research firms to inform them reliably about customer
preferences so they can tailor products to specific needs
and increase people's willingness to pay. Few end-to-end
logistics providers, which allow manufacturers to reduce
costs, are available to transport raw materials and finished products. Before recruiting employees, corporations have to screen large numbers of candidates themselves because there aren't many search firms that can
do the job for them.

Because of all those institutional voids, many multinational companies have fared poorly in developing
countries. All the anecdotal evidence we have gathered
suggests that since the 1990s, American corporations
have performed better in their home environments than
they have in foreign countries, especially in emerging
markets. Not surprisingly, many CEOs are wary of
emerging markets and prefer to invest in developed
nations instead. By the end of 2002—according to the
Bureau of Economic Analysis, an agency of the U.S.
Department of Commerce—American corporations and
their affiliate companies had $1.6 trillion worth of assets
in the United Kingdom and $514 billion in Canada but
only $173 billion in Brazil, Russia, India, and China com-
bined. That's just 2.5% of the $6.9 trillion in investments
American companies held by the end of that year. In
fact, although U.S. corporations' investments in China

doubled between 1992 and 2002, that amount was still less than 1% of all their overseas assets.

Many companies shied away from emerging markets when they should have engaged with them more closely. Since the early 1990s, developing countries have been the fastest-growing market in the world for most products and services. Companies can lower costs by setting up manufacturing facilities and service centers in those areas, where skilled labor and trained managers are relatively inexpensive. Moreover, several developing-country transnational corporations have entered North America and Europe with low-cost strategies (China's Haier Group in household electrical appliances) and novel business models (India's Infosys in information technology services). Western companies that want to develop counterstrategies must push deeper into emerging markets, which foster a different genre of innovations than mature markets do.

If Western companies don't develop strategies for engaging across their value chains with developing countries, they are unlikely to remain competitive for long. However, despite crumbling tariff barriers, the spread of the Internet and cable television, and the rapidly improving physical infrastructure in these countries, CEOs can't assume they can do business in emerging markets the same way they do in developed nations. That's because the quality of the market infrastructure varies widely from country to country. In general, advanced economies have large pools of seasoned market intermediaries and effective contract-enforcing mechanisms, whereas less-developed economies have unskilled intermediaries and less-effective legal systems. Because the services provided by intermediaries either aren't available in emerging markets or aren't very sophisticated, corporations can't smoothly transfer the strategies they employ in their home countries to those emerging markets.

During the past ten years, we've researched and consulted with multinational corporations all over the world. One of us led a comparative research project on China and India at Harvard Business School, and we have all been involved in McKinsey & Company's Global Champions research project. We have learned that successful companies work around institutional voids. They develop strategies for doing business in emerging markets that are different from those they use at home and often find novel ways of implementing them, too. They also customize their approaches to fit each nation's institutional context. As we will show, firms that take the trouble to understand the institutional differences between countries are likely to choose the best markets to enter, select optimal strategies, and make the most out of operating in emerging markets.

Why Composite Indices Are Inadequate

Before we delve deeper into institutional voids, it's important to understand why companies often target the wrong countries or deploy inappropriate globalization strategies. Many corporations enter new lands because of senior managers' personal experiences, family ties, gut feelings, or anecdotal evidence. Others follow key customers or rivals into emerging markets; the herd instinct is strong among multinationals. Biases, too, dog companies' foreign investments. For instance, the reason U.S. companies preferred to do business with China rather than India for decades was probably because of America's romance with China, first profiled in MIT political scientist Harold Isaacs's work in the late 1950s. Isaacs pointed out that partly as a result of the work missionaries and scholars did in China in the 1800s, Americans became more familiar with China than with India.

Companies that choose new markets systematically often use tools like country portfolio analysis and political risk assessment, which chiefly focus on the potential profits from doing business in developing countries but leave out essential information about the soft infrastructures there. In December 2004, when the McKinsey Global Survey of Business Executives polled 9,750 senior managers on their priorities and concerns, 61% said that market size and growth drove their firms' decisions to enter new countries. While 17% felt that political and economic stability was the most important factor in making those decisions, only 13% said that structural conditions (in other words, institutional contexts) mattered most.

Just how do companies estimate a nation's potential? Executives usually analyze its GDP and per capita income growth rates, its population composition and growth rates, and its exchange rates and purchasing power parity indices (past, present, and projected). To complete the picture, managers consider the nation's standing on the World Economic Forum's Global Competitiveness Index, the World Bank's governance indicators, and Transparency International's corruption ratings; its weight in emerging market funds investments; and, perhaps, forecasts of its next political transition.

Such composite indices are no doubt useful, but companies should use them as the basis for drawing up strategies only when their home bases and target countries have comparable institutional contexts. For example, the United States and the United Kingdom have similar product, capital, and labor markets, with networks of skilled intermediaries and strong regulatory systems. The two nations share an Anglo-Saxon legal system as well. American companies can enter Britain comfortable in the knowledge that they will find competent market research firms, that they can count on English law to enforce agreements they sign with potential partners, and that retailers will be able to distribute products all over the country. Those are dangerous assumptions to make in an emerging market, where skilled intermediaries or contract-enforcing mechanisms are unlikely to be found. However, composite indices don't flash warning signals to would-be entrants about the presence of institutional voids in emerging markets.

In fact, composite index–based analyses of developing countries conceal more than they reveal. (See the exhibit "The Trouble with Composite Indices.") In 2003, Brazil, Russia, India, and China appeared similar on several indices. Yet despite the four countries' comparable standings, the key success factors in each of those markets have turned out to be very different. For instance, in China and Russia, multinational retail chains and local retailers have expanded into the urban and semi-urban areas, whereas in Brazil, only a few global chains have set up shop in key urban centers. And in India, the government prohibited foreign direct investment in the retailing and real estate industries until February 2005, so mom-and-pop retailers dominate. Brazil, Russia, India, and China may all be big markets for multinational consumer product makers, but executives have to design unique distribution strategies for each market. That process must start with a thorough understanding of the differences between the countries' market infrastructures. Those differences may make it more attractive for some businesses to enter, say, Brazil than India.

The Trouble with Composite Indices

Companies often base their globalization strategies on country rankings, but on most lists, it is impossible to tell developing countries apart. According to the six indices below, Brazil, India, and China share similar markets, while Russia, though an outlier on many parameters, is comparable to the other nations. Contrary to what these rankings suggest, however, the market infrastructure in each of these countries varies widely, and companies need to deploy very different strategies to succeed.

	Brazil	Russia	India	China
Growth Competitiveness Index Ranking* (out of 104 countries; for 2003)	57	70	55	46
Business Competitiveness Index Ranking* (out of 103 countries; for 2003)	38	61	30	47
Governance Indicators (Percentile Rankings)** (out of 199 countries; for 2002)				
Voice and accountability	58.1	33.8	60.2	10.1
Political stability	48.1	33.0	22.2	51.4
Government effectiveness	50.0	44.3	54.1	63.4
Regulatory quality	63.4	44.3	43.8	40.2
Rule of law	50.0	25.3	57.2	51.5
Control of corruption	56.7	21.1	49.5	42.3
Corruption Perception Index Ranking*** (out of 145 countries; for 2004)	59	90	90	71
Composite Country Risk Points**** (for January 2005; the larger the number, the less risky the country)	70	78	72	76
Weight in Emerging Markets Index (%)***** (for February 2004; out of 26 emerging markets)	6.96%	5.16%	5.02%	4.76%

Sources: * World Economic Forum,"Global Competitiveness Report," 2004–2005
   ** World Bank Governance Research Indicator Country Snapshot, 2002
   *** Transparency International, Corruption Perceptions Index, 2004
   **** The PRS Group, *International Country Risk Guide*, January 2005
   ***** Barclays Global Investors, iShares "2004 Semi-Annual Report to Shareholders"

How to Map Institutional Contexts

As we helped companies think through their globalization strategies, we came up with a simple conceptual device—the five contexts framework—that lets executives map the institutional contexts of any country. Economics 101 tells us that companies buy inputs in the product, labor, and capital markets and sell their outputs in the products (raw materials and finished goods) or services market. When choosing strategies, therefore, executives need to figure out how the product, labor, and capital markets work—and don't work—in their target countries. This will help them understand the differences between home markets and those in developing countries. In addition, each country's social and political milieu—as well as the manner in which it has opened up to the outside world—shapes those markets, and companies must consider those factors, too.

The five contexts framework places a superstructure of key markets on a base of sociopolitical choices. Many multinational corporations look at either the macro factors (the degree of openness and the sociopolitical atmosphere) or some of the market factors, but few pay attention to both. We have developed sets of questions that companies can ask to create a map of each country's context and to gauge the extent to which businesses must adapt their strategies to each one. (See "Spotting Institutional Voids" at the end of this article.) Before we apply the framework to some developing countries, let's briefly touch on the five contexts.

POLITICAL AND SOCIAL SYSTEMS

As we've discussed, every country's political system affects its product, labor, and capital markets. In socialist societies like China, for instance, workers cannot form independent trade unions in the labor market, which affects wage levels. A country's social environment is also important. In South Africa, for example, the government's support for the transfer of assets to the historically disenfranchised native African community—a laudable social objective—has affected the development of the capital market. Such transfers usually price assets in an arbitrary fashion, which makes it hard for multinationals to figure out the value of South African companies and affects their assessments of potential partners.

The thorny relationships between ethnic, regional, and linguistic groups in emerging markets also affects foreign investors. In Malaysia, for instance, foreign companies should enter into joint ventures only after checking if their potential partners belong to the majority Malay community or the economically dominant Chinese community, so as not to conflict with the government's long-standing policy of transferring some assets from Chinese to Malays. This policy arose because of a perception that the race riots of 1969 were caused by the tension between the Chinese haves and the Malay have-nots. Although the rhetoric has changed somewhat in the past few years, the pro-Malay policy remains in place.

Executives would do well to identify a country's power centers, such as its bureaucracy, media, and civil society, and figure out if there are checks and balances in place. Managers must also determine how decentralized the political system is, if the government is subject to oversight, and whether bureaucrats and politicians are independent from one another. Companies should gauge the level of actual trust among the populace as opposed to enforced trust. For instance, if people believe companies won't vanish with their savings, firms may be able to raise money locally sooner rather than later.

OPENNESS

CEOs often talk about the need for economies to be open because they believe it's best to enter countries that welcome direct investment by multinational corporations—although companies can get into countries that don't allow foreign investment by entering into joint ventures or by licensing local partners. Still, they must remember that the concept of "open" can be deceptive. For example, executives believe that China is an open economy because the government welcomes foreign investment but that India is a relatively closed economy because of the lukewarm reception the Indian government gives multinationals. However, India has been open to ideas from the West, and people have always been able to travel freely in and out of the country, whereas for decades, the Chinese government didn't allow its citizens to travel abroad freely, and it still doesn't allow many ideas to cross its borders. Consequently, while it may be true that multinational companies can invest in China more easily than they can in India, managers in India are more inclined to be market oriented and globally aware than managers are in China.

The more open a country's economy, the more likely it is that global intermediaries will be allowed to operate there. Multinationals, therefore, will find it easier to function in markets that are more open because they can use the services of both the global and local intermediaries. However, openness can be a double-edged sword: A government that allows local companies to access the global capital market neutralizes one of foreign companies' key advantages.

The two macro contexts we have just described—political and social systems and openness—shape the market contexts. For instance, in Chile, a military coup in the early 1970s led to the establishment of a right-wing government, and that government's liberal economic policies led to a vibrant capital market in the country. But Chile's labor market remained underdeveloped because the government did not allow trade unions to operate freely. Similarly, openness affects the development of markets. If a country's capital markets are open to foreign investors, financial intermediaries will become more sophisticated. That has happened in India, for example, where capital markets are more open than they are in China. Likewise, in the product market, if multinationals can invest in the retail industry, logistics providers will develop rapidly. This has been the case in China, where providers have taken hold more quickly than they have in India, which has only recently allowed multinationals to invest in retailing.

PRODUCT MARKETS

Developing countries have opened up their markets and grown rapidly during the past decade, but companies still struggle to get reliable information about consumers, especially those with low incomes. Developing a consumer finance business is tough, for example, because the data sources and credit histories that firms draw on in the West don't exist in emerging markets. Market research and advertising are in their infancy in developing countries, and it's difficult to find the deep databases on consumption patterns that allow compa-

nies to segment consumers in more-developed markets.
There are few government bodies or independent publications, like *Consumer Reports* in the United States, that
provide expert advice on the features and quality of
products. Because of a lack of consumer courts and
advocacy groups in developing nations, many people feel
they are at the mercy of big companies.

LABOR MARKETS

In spite of emerging markets' large populations, multinationals have trouble recruiting managers and other
skilled workers because the quality of talent is hard to
ascertain. There are relatively few search firms and
recruiting agencies in low-income countries. The high-
quality firms that do exist focus on top-level searches, so
companies must scramble to identify middle-level managers, engineers, or floor supervisors. Engineering col-
leges, business schools, and training institutions have
proliferated, but apart from an elite few, there's no way
for companies to tell which schools produce skilled managers. For instance, several Indian companies have
sprung up to train people for jobs in the call center
business, but no organization rates the quality of the
training it provides.

CAPITAL MARKETS

The capital and financial markets in developing countries
are remarkable for their lack of sophistication. Apart
from a few stock exchanges and government-appointed
regulators, there aren't many reliable intermediaries like
credit-rating agencies, investment analysts, merchant
bankers, or venture capital firms. Multinationals can't

count on raising debt or equity capital locally to finance their operations. Like investors, creditors don't have access to accurate information on companies. Businesses can't easily assess the creditworthiness of other firms or collect receivables after they have extended credit to customers. Corporate governance is also notoriously poor in emerging markets. Transnational companies, therefore, can't trust their partners to adhere to local laws and joint venture agreements. In fact, since crony capitalism thrives in developing countries, multinationals can't assume that the profit motive alone is what's driving local firms.

Several CEOs have asked us why we emphasize the role of institutional intermediaries and ignore industry factors. They argue that industry structure, such as the degree of competition, should also influence companies' strategies. But when Harvard Business School professor Jan Rivkin and one of the authors of this article ranked industries by profitability, they found that the correlation of industry rankings across pairs of countries was close to zero, which means that the attractiveness of an industry varied widely from country to country. So although factors like scale economies, entry barriers, and the ability to differentiate products matter in every industry, the weight of their importance varies from place to place. An attractive industry in your home market may turn out to be unattractive in another country. Companies should analyze industry structures—always a useful exercise—only after they understand a country's institutional context.

Applying the Framework

When we applied the five contexts framework to emerging markets in four countries—Brazil, Russia, India, and

China—the differences between them became apparent. (See the exhibit "Mapping Contexts in Brazil, Russia, India, and China.") Multinationals face different kinds of competition in each of those nations. In China, state-owned enterprises control nearly half the economy, members of the Chinese diaspora control many of the foreign corporations that operate there, and the private sector brings up the rear because entrepreneurs find it almost impossible to access capital. India is the mirror image of China. Public sector corporations, though important, occupy nowhere near as prominent a place as they do in China. Unlike China, India is wary of foreign investment, even by members of the Indian diaspora. However, the country has spawned many private sector organizations, some of which are globally competitive. It's difficult to imagine a successful business in China that hasn't had something to do with the government; in India, most companies have succeeded in spite of the state.

Brazil mixes and matches features of both China and India. Like China, Brazil has floated many state-owned enterprises. At the same time, it has kept its doors open to multinationals, and European corporations such as Unilever, Volkswagen, and Nestlé have been able to build big businesses there. Volkswagen has six plants in Brazil, dominates the local market, and exports its Gol model to Argentina and Russia. Brazil also boasts private sector companies that, like Indian firms, go head-to-head in the local market with global firms. Some Brazilian companies, such as basic materials company Votorantim and aircraft maker Embraer, have become globally competitive.

Russia is also a cross between China and India, but most of its companies are less competitive than those in Brazil. A few multinationals such as McDonald's

Mapping Contexts in Brazil, Russia, India, and China

The five contexts (below) can help companies spot the institutional voids in any country. An application of the framework to the four fastest-growing markets in the world reveals how different those countries are from developed nations and, more important, from one another.

POLITICAL AND SOCIAL SYSTEM

Political Structure

U.S./EU   Countries have vibrant democracies with checks and balances. Companies can count on rule of law and fair enforcement of legal contracts.

Brazil   The democracy is vibrant. Bureaucracy is rampant. There are pockets of corruption in federal and state governments.

Russia   A centralized government and some regional fiefdoms coexist. Bureaucracy is stifling. Corruption occurs at all levels of government.

India   The democracy is vibrant. The government is highly bureaucratic. Corruption is rampant in state and local governments.

China   The Communist Party maintains a monopoly on political power. Local governments make economic policy decisions. Officials may abuse power for personal gain.

Civil Society

U.S./EU   A dynamic media acts as a check on abuses by both companies and governments. Powerful nongovernmental organizations (NGOs) influence corporate policies on social and environmental issues.

Brazil   Influential local media serves as a watchdog. The influence of local NGOs is marginal.

Russia   The media is controlled by the government. NGOs are underdeveloped and disorganized.

India   A dynamic press and vigilant NGOs act as checks on politicians and companies.

China   The media is muzzled by the government, and there are few independent NGOs. Companies don't have to worry about criticism, but they can't count on civil society to check abuses of power.

OPENNESS

Modes of Entry

U.S./EU	Open to all forms of foreign investment except when governments have concerns about potential monopolies or national security issues.
Brazil	Both greenfield investments and acquisitions are possible entry strategies. Companies team up with local partners to gain local expertise.
Russia	Both greenfield investments and acquisitions are possible but difficult. Companies form alliances to gain access to government and local inputs.
India	Restrictions on greenfield investments and acquisitions in some sectors make joint ventures necessary. Red tape hinders companies in sectors where the government does allow foreign investment.
China	The government permits greenfield investments as well as acquisitions. Acquired companies are likely to have been state owned and may have hidden liabilities. Alliances let companies align interests with all levels of government.

PRODUCT MARKETS

Product Development and Intellectual Property Rights (IPR)

U.S./EU	Sophisticated product-design capabilities are available. Governments enforce IPR and protect trademarks, so R&D investments yield competitive advantages.
Brazil	Local design capability exists. IPR disputes with the United States exist in some sectors.
Russia	The country has a strong local design capability but exhibits an ambivalent attitude about IPR. Sufficient regulatory authority exists, but enforcement is patchy.
India	Some local design capability is available. IPR problems with the United States exist in some industries. Regulatory bodies monitor product quality and fraud.

(continued)

China   Imitation and piracy abound. Punishment for IPR theft varies across provinces and by level of corruption.

Supplier Base and Logistics

U.S./EU   Companies use national and international suppliers. Firms outsource and move manufacturing and services offshore instead of integrating vertically. A highly developed infrastructure is in place, but urban areas are saturated.

Brazil   Suppliers are available in the Mercosur region. A good network of highways, airports, and ports exists.

Russia   Companies can rely on local suppliers for simple components. The European region has decent logistics networks, but trans-Ural Russia is not well developed.

India   Suppliers are available, but their quality and dependability varies greatly. Roads are in poor condition. Ports and airports are underdeveloped.

China   Several suppliers have strong manufacturing capabilities, but few vendors have advanced technical abilities. The road network is well developed. Port facilities are excellent.

Brand Perceptions and Management

U.S./EU   Markets are mature and have strong local and global brands. The profusion of brands clutters consumer choice. Numerous ad agencies are available.

Brazil   Consumers accept both local and global brands. Global as well as local ad agencies are present.

Russia   Consumers prefer global brands in automobiles and high tech. Local brands thrive in the food and beverage businesses. Some local and global ad agencies are available.

India   Consumers buy both local and global brands. Global ad agencies are present, but they have been less successful than local ad agencies.

China   Consumers prefer to buy products from American, European, and Japanese companies. Multinational ad agencies dominate the business.

LABOR MARKETS

Market for Managers

U.S./EU A large and varied pool of well-trained management talent exists.

Brazil The large pool of management talent has varying degrees of proficiency in English. Both local and expatriate managers hold senior management jobs.

Russia The large pool of management talent has varying degrees of proficiency in English, and it is supplemented by expatriate managers. Employment agencies are booming.

India The country has a highly liquid pool of English-speaking management talent fueled by business and technical schools. Local hires are preferred over expatriates.

China There is a relatively small and static market for managers, especially away from the eastern seaboard. Many senior and middle managers aren't fluent in English. A large number of managers are expatriates. Some members of the Chinese diaspora have returned home to work.

Workers Market

U.S./EU The level of unionization varies among countries. Industrial actions take place in Europe, especially in the manufacturing and public sectors, but not in the United States.

Brazil Trade unions are strong and pragmatic, which means that companies can sign agreements with them.

Russia Trade unions are present, but their influence is declining except in certain sectors, such as mining and railways.

India The trade union movement is active and volatile, although it is becoming less important. Trade unions have strong political connections.

China Workers can join the government-controlled All-China Federation of Trade Unions. Historically, there were no industrial actions, but there have been recent strikes at Hong Kong– and Taiwan-owned manufacturing facilities.

(continued)

CAPITAL MARKETS

Debt and Equity

U.S./EU   Companies can easily get bank loans. The corporate bond market is well developed. The integration of stock exchanges gives companies access to a deep pool of investors.

Brazil   A good banking system exists, and there is a healthy market for initial public offerings. Wealthy individuals can invest in offshore accounts.

Russia   The banking system is strong but dominated by state-owned banks. The consumer credit market is booming, and the IPO market is growing. Firms must incorporate local subsidiaries to raise equity capital.

India   The local banking system is well developed. Multinationals can rely on local banks for local needs. Equity is available to local and foreign entities.

China   The local banking system and equity markets are underdeveloped. Foreign companies have to raise both debt and equity in home markets.

Venture Capital (VC)

U.S./EU   VC is generally available in urban areas or for specific industry clusters. VC is not as readily available in southern Europe.

Brazil   A few private equity players are active locally.

Russia   Only companies in the most profitable businesses, such as real estate development and natural resources, can access VC.

India   VC is available in some cities and from the Indian diaspora.

China   VC availability is limited.

Accounting Standards

U.S./EU   Apart from off-balance-sheet items, a high level of transparency exists. In the European Union, accounting practices should become more uniform after 2005 because of new norms.

Brazil   The financial-reporting system is based on a common-law system and functions well.

Russia   The modified Soviet system of financial reporting works well. Banks are shifting to international accounting standards.

India	Financial reporting, which is based on a common-law system, functions well.
China	There is little corporate transparency. China's accounting standards are not strict, although the China Securities Regulatory Commission wants to tighten disclosure rules.

Financial Distress

U.S./EU	Efficient bankruptcy processes tend to favor certain stakeholders (creditors, labor force, or shareholders) in certain countries.
Brazil	Processes allow companies to stay in business rather than go out of business. Bankruptcy processes exist but are inefficient.
Russia	Bankruptcy processes and legislation are fully developed. Corruption distorts bankruptcy enforcement.
India	Bankruptcy processes exist but are inefficient. Promoters find it difficult to sell off or shut down "sick" enterprises.
China	Companies can use bankruptcy processes in some cases. Write-offs are common.

Source: Media reports and interviews with academics and businesspeople.

have done well, but most foreign firms have failed to make headway there. There are only a few strong private sector companies in the market, such as dairy products maker Wimm-Bill-Dann and cellular services provider VimpelCom. The Russian government is involved, formally and informally, in several industries. For instance, the government's equity stake in Gazprom allows it to influence the country's energy sector. Moreover, administrators at all levels can exercise near veto power over business deals that involve local or foreign companies, and getting permits and approvals is a complicated chore in Russia.

One level deeper, the financial markets in Brazil, Russia, India, and China vary, too. In Brazil and India, indigenous entrepreneurs, who are multinationals' main rivals, rely on the local capital markets for resources. In China, foreign companies compete with state-owned enterprises, which public sector banks usually fund. The difference is important because neither the Chinese companies nor the banks are under pressure to show profits. Moreover, financial reporting in China isn't transparent even if companies have listed themselves on stock exchanges. State-owned companies can for years pursue strategies that increase their market share at the expense of profits. Corporate governance standards in Brazil and India also mimic those of the West more closely than do those in Russia and China. Thus, in Russia and China, multinationals can't count on local partners' internal systems to protect their interests and assets—especially their intellectual property.

The Three Strategy Choices

When companies tailor strategies to each country's contexts, they can capitalize on the strengths of particular locations. Before adapting their approaches, however, firms must compare the benefits of doing so with the additional coordination costs they'll incur. When they complete this exercise, companies will find that they have three distinct choices: They can adapt their business model to countries while keeping their core value propositions constant, they can try to change the contexts, or they can stay out of countries where adapting strategies may be uneconomical or impractical. Can companies sustain strategies that presume the existence of institutional voids? They can. It took decades to fill institutional voids in the West.

ADAPT YOUR STRATEGIES

To succeed, multinationals must modify their business models for each nation. They may have to adapt to the voids in a country's product markets, its input markets, or both. But companies must retain their core business propositions even as they adapt their business models. If they make shifts that are too radical, these firms will lose their advantages of global scale and global branding.

Compare Dell's business models in the United States and China. In the United States, the hardware maker offers consumers a wide variety of configurations and makes most computers to order. Dell doesn't use distributors or resellers, shipping most machines directly to buyers. In 2003, nearly 50% of the company's revenues in North America came from orders placed through the Internet.

The cornerstone of Dell's business model is that it carries little or no inventory. But Dell realized that its direct-sales approach wouldn't work in China, because individuals weren't accustomed to buying PCs through the Internet. Chinese companies used paper-based order processing, so Dell had to rely on faxes and phones rather than online sales. And several Chinese government departments and state-owned enterprises insisted that hardware vendors make their bids through systems integrators. The upshot is that Dell relies heavily on distributors and systems integrators in China. When it first entered the market there, the company offered a smaller product range than it did in the United States to keep inventory levels low. Later, as its supply chain became more efficient, it offered customers in China a full range of products.

Smart companies like Dell modify their business model without destroying the parts of it that give them a competitive advantage over rivals. These firms start by identifying the value propositions that they will not modify, whatever the context. That's what McDonald's did even as it comprehensively adapted its business model to Russia's factor markets. In the United States, McDonald's has outsourced most of its supply chain operations. But when it tried to move into Russia in 1990, the company was unable to find local suppliers. The fast-food chain asked several of its European vendors to step up, but they weren't interested. Instead of giving up, McDonald's decided to go it alone. With the help of its joint venture partner, the Moscow City Administration, the company identified some Russian farmers and bakers it could work with. It imported cattle from Holland and russet potatoes from America, brought in agricultural specialists from Canada and Europe to improve the farmers' management practices, and advanced the farmers money so that they could invest in better seeds and equipment.

Then the company built a 100,000 square-foot McComplex in Moscow to produce beef; bakery, potato, and dairy products; ketchup; mustard; and Big Mac sauce. It set up a trucking fleet to move supplies to restaurants and financed its suppliers so that they would have enough working capital to buy modern equipment. The company also brought in about 50 expatriate managers to teach Russian employees about its service standards, quality measurements, and operating procedures and sent a 23-person team of Russian managers to Canada for a four-month training program. McDonald's created a vertically integrated operation in Russia, but the company clung to one principle:

It would sell only hamburgers, fries, and Coke to Russians in a clean environment—fast. Fifteen years after serving its first Big Mac in Moscow's Pushkin Square, McDonald's has invested $250 million in the country and controls 80% of the Russian fast-food market.

CHANGE THE CONTEXTS

Many multinationals are powerful enough to alter the contexts in which they operate. The products or services these companies offer can force dramatic changes in local markets. When Asia's first satellite TV channel, Hong Kong–based STAR, launched in 1991, for example, it transformed the Indian marketplace in many ways. Not only did the company cause the Indian government to lose its monopoly on television broadcasts overnight, but it also led to a booming TV-manufacturing industry and the launch of several other satellite-based channels aimed at Indian audiences. By the mid-1990s, satellite-based TV channels had become a vibrant advertising medium, and many organizations used them to launch products and services targeted at India's new TV-watching consumer class.

The entry of foreign companies transforms quality standards in local product markets, which can have far-reaching consequences. Japan's Suzuki triggered a quality revolution after it entered India in 1981. The automaker's need for large volumes of high-quality components roused local suppliers. They teamed up with Suzuki's vendors in Japan, formed quality clusters, and worked with Japanese experts to produce better products. During the next two decades, the total quality management movement spread to other industries in India. By 2004, Indian companies had bagged more Deming prizes than firms in any country other than Japan. More important, India's automotive suppliers had succeeded in breaking into the global market, and several of them, such as Sundram Fasteners, had become preferred suppliers to international automakers like GM.

Companies can change contexts in factor markets, too. Consider the capital market in Brazil. As multinationals set up subsidiaries in those countries, they needed global-quality audit services. Few Brazilian accounting firms could provide those services, so the Big Four audit firms—Deloitte Touche Tohmatsu, Ernst & Young, KPMG, and PricewaterhouseCoopers—decided to set up branches there. The presence of those companies quickly raised financial-reporting and auditing standards in Brazil.

In a similar vein, Knauf, one of Europe's leading manufacturers of building materials, is trying to grow Russia's talent market. During the past decade, the German giant has built 20 factories in Russia and invested more than $400 million there. Knauf operates in a people-intensive industry; the company and its subsidiaries have roughly 7,000 employees in Russia. To boost standards in the country's construction industry, Knauf opened an education center in St. Petersburg in 2003 that works closely with the State Architectural and Construction University. The school acts both as a mechanism that supplies talent to Knauf and as an institution that contributes to the much-needed development of Russian architecture.

Indeed, as firms change contexts, they must help countries fully develop their potential. That creates a win-win situation for the country and the company. Metro Cash & Carry, a division of German trading company Metro Group, has changed contexts in a socially beneficial way in several European and Asian countries.

The Düsseldorf-based company—which sells everything to restaurants from meats and vegetables to napkins and toothpicks—entered China in 1996, Russia in 2001, and India in 2003. Metro has pioneered business links between farmers and small-scale manufacturers in rural areas that sell their products to small and midsize urban companies.

For instance, Metro invested in a cold chain in China so that it could deliver goods like fish and meats from rural regions to urban locations. That changed local conditions in several important ways. First, Metro's investment induced farmers in China to invest more in their agricultural operations. Metro also lobbied with governments for quality standards to prevent companies from selling shoddy produce to hapless consumers. By shifting transactions from roadside markets to computerized warehouses, the company's operations brought primary products into the tax net. Governments, which need the money to invest in local services, have remained on the company's side. That's a good thing for Metro since, in developing markets, the jury is always out on foreign companies.

STAY AWAY

It may be impractical or uneconomical for some firms to adapt their business models to emerging markets. Home Depot, the successful do-it-yourself U.S. retailer, has been cautious about entering developing countries. The company offers a specific value proposition to customers: low prices, great service, and good quality. To pull that off, it relies on a variety of U.S.-specific institutions. It depends on the U.S. highways and logistical management systems to minimize the amount of inventory it has to carry in its large, warehouse-style stores. It relies on employee stock ownership to motivate shop-level workers to render top-notch service. And its value proposition takes advantage of the fact that high labor costs in the United States encourage home owners to engage in do-it-yourself projects.

Home Depot made a tentative foray into emerging markets by setting up two stores in Chile in 1998 and another in Argentina in 2000. In 2001, however, the company sold those operations for a net loss of $14 million. At the time, CEO Robert Nardelli emphasized that most of Home Depot's future growth was likely to come from North America. Despite that initial setback, the company hasn't entirely abandoned emerging markets. Rather, it has switched from a greenfield strategy to an acquisition-led approach. In 2001, Home Depot entered Mexico by buying a home improvement retailer, Total Home, and the next year, it acquired Del Norte, another small chain. By 2004, the company had 42 stores in Mexico. Although Home Depot has recently said that it is exploring the possibility of entering China, perhaps by making an acquisition, it doesn't have retail operations in any other developing countries.

Home Depot must consider whether it can modify its U.S. business model to suit the institutional contexts of emerging markets. In a country with a poorly developed capital market, for example, the company may not be able to use employee stock ownership as a compensation tool. Similarly, in a country with a poorly developed physical infrastructure, Home Depot may have difficulty using its inventory management systems, a scenario that would alter the economics of the business. In markets where labor costs are relatively low, the target customer may not be the home owner but rather contractors who serve as intermediaries between the store and the home owner. That change in customer focus may warrant an entirely different marketing and merchandising strategy—one that Home Depot isn't convinced it should deploy yet.

WHILE COMPANIES CAN'T USE the same strategies in all developing countries, they can generate synergies by treating different markets as part of a system. For instance, GE Healthcare (formerly GE Medical Systems) makes parts for its diagnostic machines in China, Hungary, and Mexico and develops the software for those machines in India. The company created this system when it realized that the market for diagnostic machines was small in most low-income countries. GE Healthcare then decided to use the facility it had set up in India in 1990 as a global sourcing base. After several years, and on the back of borrowed expertise from GE Japan, the India operation's products finally met GE Healthcare's exacting standards. In the late 1990s, when GE Healthcare wanted to move a plant from Belgium to cut costs, the Indian subsidiary beat its Mexican counterpart by delivering the highest quality at the lowest cost. Under its then-CEO, Jeff Immelt, GE Healthcare learned to use all its operations in low-income countries—China, Hungary, Mexico, and India—as parts of a system that allowed the company to produce equipment cheaply for the world market.

Parent company GE has also tapped into the talent pool in emerging markets by setting up technology centers in Shanghai and Bangalore, for instance. In those centers, the company conducts research on everything from materials design to molecular modeling to power electronics. GE doesn't treat China and India just as markets but also as sources of talent and innovation that can transform its value chain. And that's how multinational companies should engage with emerging markets if they wish to secure their future.

Spotting Institutional Voids

MANAGERS CAN IDENTIFY the institutional voids in any country by asking a series of questions. The answers—or sometimes, the lack of them—will tell companies where they should adapt their business models to the nation's institutional context.

Political and Social System

1. To whom are the country's politicians accountable? Are there strong political groups that oppose the ruling party? Do elections take place regularly?

2. Are the roles of the legislative, executive, and judiciary clearly defined? What is the distribution of power between the central, state, and city governments?

3. Does the government go beyond regulating business to interfering in it or running companies?

4. Do the laws articulate and protect private property rights?

5. What is the quality of the country's bureaucrats? What are bureaucrats' incentives and career trajectories?

6. Is the judiciary independent? Do the courts adjudicate disputes and enforce contracts in a timely and impartial manner? How effective are the quasi-judicial regulatory institutions that set and enforce rules for business activities?

7. Do religious, linguistic, regional, and ethnic groups co-exist peacefully, or are there tensions between them?

8. How vibrant and independent is the media? Are newspapers and magazines neutral, or do they represent sectarian interests?

9. Are nongovernmental organizations, civil rights groups, and environmental groups active in the country?

10. Do people tolerate corruption in business and government?

11. What role do family ties play in business?

12. Can strangers be trusted to honor a contract in the country?

Openness

1. Are the country's government, media, and people receptive to foreign investment? Do citizens trust companies and individuals from some parts of the world more than others?

2. What restrictions does the government place on foreign investment? Are those restrictions in place to facilitate the growth of domestic companies, to protect state monopolies, or because people are suspicious of multinationals?

3. Can a company make greenfield investments and acquire local companies, or can it only break into the market by entering into joint ventures? Will that company be free to choose partners based purely on economic considerations?

4. Does the country allow the presence of foreign intermediaries such as market research and advertising firms, retailers, media companies, banks, insurance companies, venture capital firms, auditing firms, management consulting firms, and educational institutions?

5. How long does it take to start a new venture in the country? How cumbersome are the government's procedures for permitting the launch of a wholly foreign-owned business?

6. Are there restrictions on portfolio investments by overseas companies or on dividend repatriation by multinationals?

7. Does the market drive exchange rates, or does the government control them? If it's the latter, does the government try to maintain a stable exchange rate, or does it try to favor domestic products over imports by propping up the local currency?

8. What would be the impact of tariffs on a company's capital goods and raw materials imports? How would import duties affect that company's ability to manufacture its products locally versus exporting them from home?

9. Can a company set up its business anywhere in the country? If the government restricts the company's location choices, are its motives political, or is it inspired by a logical regional development strategy?

10. Has the country signed free-trade agreements with other nations? If so, do those agreements favor investments by companies from some parts of the world over others?

11. Does the government allow foreign executives to enter and leave the country freely? How difficult is it to get work permits for managers and engineers?

12. Does the country allow its citizens to travel abroad freely? Can ideas flow into the country unrestricted? Are people permitted to debate and accept those ideas?

Product Markets

1. Can companies easily obtain reliable data on customer tastes and purchase behaviors? Are there cultural barriers

to market research? Do world-class market research firms operate in the country?

2. Can consumers easily obtain unbiased information on the quality of the goods and services they want to buy? Are there independent consumer organizations and publications that provide such information?

3. Can companies access raw materials and components of good quality? Is there a deep network of suppliers? Are there firms that assess suppliers' quality and reliability? Can companies enforce contracts with suppliers?

4. How strong are the logistics and transportation infrastructures? Have global logistics companies set up local operations?

5. Do large retail chains exist in the country? If so, do they cover the entire country or only the major cities? Do they reach all consumers or only wealthy ones?

6. Are there other types of distribution channels, such as direct-to-consumer channels and discount retail channels, that deliver products to customers?

7. Is it difficult for multinationals to collect receivables from local retailers?

8. Do consumers use credit cards, or does cash dominate transactions? Can consumers get credit to make purchases? Are data on customer creditworthiness available?

9. What recourse do consumers have against false claims by companies or defective products and services?

10. How do companies deliver after-sales service to consumers? Is it possible to set up a nationwide service network? Are third-party service providers reliable?

11. Are consumers willing to try new products and services? Do they trust goods from local companies? How about from foreign companies?

12. What kind of product-related environmental and safety regulations are in place? How do the authorities enforce those regulations?

Labor Markets

1. How strong is the country's education infrastructure, especially for technical and management training? Does it have a good elementary and secondary education system as well?

2. Do people study and do business in English or in another international language, or do they mainly speak a local language?

3. Are data available to help sort out the quality of the country's educational institutions?

4. Can employees move easily from one company to another? Does the local culture support that movement? Do recruitment agencies facilitate executive mobility?

5. What are the major postrecruitment-training needs of the people that multinationals hire locally?

6. Is pay for performance a standard practice? How much weight do executives give seniority, as opposed to merit, in making promotion decisions?

7. Would a company be able to enforce employment contracts with senior executives? Could it protect itself against executives who leave the firm and then compete against it? Could it stop employees from stealing trade secrets and intellectual property?

8. Does the local culture accept foreign managers? Do the laws allow a firm to transfer locally hired people to

another country? Do managers want to stay or leave the nation?

9. How are the rights of workers protected? How strong are the country's trade unions? Do they defend workers' interests or only advance a political agenda?

10. Can companies use stock options and stock-based compensation schemes to motivate employees?

11. Do the laws and regulations limit a firm's ability to restructure, downsize, or shut down?

12. If a company were to adopt its local rivals' or suppliers' business practices, such as the use of child labor, would that tarnish its image overseas?

Capital Markets

1. How effective are the country's banks, insurance companies, and mutual funds at collecting savings and channeling them into investments?

2. Are financial institutions managed well? Is their decision making transparent? Do noneconomic considerations, such as family ties, influence their investment decisions?

3. Can companies raise large amounts of equity capital in the stock market? Is there a market for corporate debt?

4. Does a venture capital industry exist? If so, does it allow individuals with good ideas to raise funds?

5. How reliable are sources of information on company performance? Do the accounting standards and disclosure regulations permit investors and creditors to monitor company management?

6. Do independent financial analysts, rating agencies, and the media offer unbiased information on companies?

7. How effective are corporate governance norms and standards at protecting shareholder interests?

8. Are corporate boards independent and empowered, and do they have independent directors?

9. Are regulators effective at monitoring the banking industry and stock markets?

10. How well do the courts deal with fraud?

11. Do the laws permit companies to engage in hostile takeovers? Can shareholders organize themselves to remove entrenched managers through proxy fights?

12. Is there an orderly bankruptcy process that balances the interests of owners, creditors, and other stakeholders?

Originally published in June 2005
Reprint R0506C

Andy Klump, Niraj Kaji, Luis Sanchez, and Max Yacoub provided research assistance for the Dell and McDonald's examples in this article.

Emerging Giants

Building World-Class Companies in Developing Countries

TARUN KHANNA AND KRISHNA G. PALEPU

Executive Summary

OVER THE PAST 20 YEARS, waves of liberalization
have all but washed away protectionist barriers in developing countries. As multinational corporations from North
America, Western Europe, Japan, and South Korea
stormed into the emerging markets, many local companies lost market share or sold off businesses—but some
fought back. India's Mahindra & Mahindra, China's
Haier Group, and many other corporations in developing countries have held their own against the onslaught,
restructured their businesses, exploited new opportunities,
and built world-class companies that are today giving
their global rivals a run for their money.

In this article, the authors, citing the results of their six-
year study of "emerging giants," describe the three strategies these businesses used to become effective global
competitors—despite facing financial and bureaucratic
disadvantages in their home markets.

131

Some capitalized on their *knowledge of local product markets.* The Philippines' Jollibee Foods, for instance, has profitably battled McDonald's because it realizes that Filipinos like their burgers to have a particular soy and garlic taste.

Some have exploited their *knowledge of local talent and capital markets,* thereby serving customers both at home and abroad in a cost-effective manner. India's software companies, for instance, recognized the possibility of providing services to overseas customers at least a decade before Western companies even considered hiring Indian software professionals.

And some emerging giants have exploited *institutional voids* to create profitable businesses. China's Emerge Logistics, for instance, helps foreign companies navigate the country's disjointed transportation system and baffling bureaucracy, guiding them all the way from ports to retail outlets.

The authors' research indicates there's more than one way to skin the proverbial cat: Some emerging-market companies compete in several countries, but others sell only at home. Emerging giants can be successful even if they don't have global footprints, Khanna and Palepu conclude.

IN 2003, just months after Mahindra & Mahindra launched a smartly designed sport-utility vehicle called the Scorpio, CNBC India, BBC World's *Wheels* program, and others were heaping Car of the Year awards on the SUV. That was no mean achievement: The made-in-India automobile won top honors ahead of global best sellers such as the Mercedes-Benz E-Class and Toyota Camry sedans. To M&M, which manufactures tractors in several countries as well as vehicles targeted at India's semi-urban and rural markets, the awards signaled that it could finally take the world's automakers head-on. Even as the Scorpio successfully battles multipurpose vehicles like Toyota's Innova and GM's Chevy Tavera at home, M&M has started marketing the SUV in South Africa and Spain. Clearly, the $1.73 billion Indian company is on the road to becoming a player in the global automobile industry.

M&M isn't the only company from an emerging market that is making the world sit up and take notice.

Over the past two-plus decades, waves of liberalization have all but washed away protectionist barriers in developing countries. As those nations integrated themselves into the world economy, multinational corporations from North America, Western Europe, Japan, and South Korea stormed in. Many local companies lost market share or sold off businesses as a result, but some fought back. They held their own against the onslaught, restructured their businesses, exploited new opportunities, and built world-class companies that today are giving their global rivals a run for their money.

Some emerging giants compete in several countries—for instance, Brazil's AmBev (which in 2004 merged with Belgium's Interbrew to form InBev); Chile's S.A.C.I. Falabella; China's Baosteel, Galanz, and Lenovo groups and Huawei Technologies; India's Dr. Reddy's Laboratories, Infosys, NIIT, Ranbaxy, Satyam, Tata Group, and Wipro; Israel's Teva Pharmaceuticals; Mexico's Cemex; the Philippines' Jollibee Foods; and South Africa's SABMiller. Others operate mainly at home—for example, China's Wahaha Group; India's Bharti Tele-Ventures and ITC Limited; and Turkey's Koç and Doğuş business groups.

What strategies did these globally competitive businesses deploy to overcome the myriad obstacles that their home environments pose? Why and how did some of them move from their dominant positions at home to establish an international presence? Must every emerging-market company follow suit? What sequence of steps should wannabe giants take to build stronger businesses at home or to enter markets overseas?

Six years ago, we decided to study several companies in developing countries as they created global businesses and emerged on the world stage. Academics such as Harvard Business School's Louis T. Wells, Jr. (who in 1983 popularized the term "Third World multinationals") and MIT's Alice H. Amsden (who in 2000 called firms in emerging markets "companies that rise from the rest") have studied similar businesses. Our focus, however, wasn't on the role that economic policy plays in creating globally competitive companies but on strategies and business models. That's important; several countries have opened up to foreign competition over the years, which has recast the challenges companies in emerging markets face: Survival is tougher, but the opportunities are more enticing than ever. We identified 134 major companies in ten emerging markets—Argentina, Brazil, Chile, China, India, Indonesia, Mexico, Poland, South Africa, and Turkey—and analyzed data on each company, from its strategies to its stock market performance. The patterns, you'll find, are intriguing.

Blunting the Multinationals' Edge

At first glance, Western, Japanese, and South Korean companies appear to hold near-insurmountable advantages over businesses in newly industrializing countries.

They not only possess well-known brand names, efficient innovation processes and management systems, and sophisticated technologies but also have access to vast reservoirs of finance and talent. Western European and American companies, for instance, can raise large sums of money at a low cost because of their well-established financial markets. They can hire talent easily because the labor markets on both continents work well. Most developing countries lack the soft infrastructure that makes markets work efficiently, as we have pointed out in previous *Harvard Business Review* articles. (See, for instance, "Why Focused Strategies May Be Wrong for Emerging Markets," July–August 1997.) Because of institutional voids—the absence of specialized intermediaries, regulatory systems, and contract-enforcing mechanisms—corporations in emerging markets cannot access capital or talent as easily or as inexpensively as European and American corporations can. That often makes it tough for businesses in developing countries to invest in R&D or to build global brands.

Nevertheless, these companies can overcome such disadvantages, for three reasons. First, when multinational companies from the developed world explore business opportunities in emerging markets, they must confront the same institutional voids that local companies face. However, executives from multinational companies are used to operating in economies with well-developed institutional infrastructures and are therefore ill equipped to deal with such voids. Western organizations, for instance, rely on data from market research firms to tailor their products and marketing strategies to compete in different markets. They also count on supply chain partners to make and deliver products to customers inexpensively. When these companies attempt to move into countries that don't have sophisticated market researchers or reliable supply chain partners, they find it difficult to deploy their business models. By contrast, the managers at local companies know how to work around institutional voids because they've had years of experience doing so. Their familiarity with the local context allows them to identify and meet customers' needs effectively. Moreover, business groups such as India's Tata Group, the Philippines' Ayala Group, and Turkey's Koç Group have created mechanisms for raising capital and developing talent. They can, for instance, raise money from the local stock market by trading on their reputations. These groups can also spread the cost of training executives in-house by deploying their managers across businesses. Such mechanisms allow many local companies to compete effectively with foreign giants.

Second, once companies from emerging markets have demonstrated a degree of success, they, too, can tap capital and talent markets in developed countries. Like American and European companies, they can raise money by, say, listing themselves on the New York Stock Exchange or on Nasdaq. Emerging giants often become investors' darlings, making it easy for them to sell equity shares or bonds. In the talent market, intermediaries from developed countries that are trying to fill the gaps in the soft infrastructure in emerging markets help local businesses become more competitive. In recent years, American and European business schools have launched education programs in developing countries. This has allowed emerging-market companies to retrain their existing managers and to hire people with the same skills that executives in multinational companies possess.

Third—and this is often downplayed by executives—multinational companies are reluctant, sometimes rightly so, to tailor their strategies to every developing market in which they operate. They find it costly and cumbersome to modify their products, services, and communications to suit local tastes, especially since the opportunities in developing countries tend to be relatively small and risky. Further, their organizational processes and cost structures make it difficult for them to sell products and services at optimal price points in emerging markets; they often end up occupying small, superpremium niches. Local companies don't suffer from those constraints, particularly since they operate in just a few geographic markets. In fact, we've found that once emerging-market companies improve the quality of their products and services, they are able to cater to customers at home as well as, if not better than, multinational companies.

Market Structures in Developing Countries

The structure of markets in developing countries helps local companies counter their multinational rivals. Most product markets comprise four distinct tiers: a global customer segment that wants products of global quality and with global features—that is, offerings with the same quality and attributes that goods in developed countries have—and is willing to pay global prices for them; a "glocal" segment that demands products of global quality but with local features (and local soul) at less-than-global prices; a local segment that wants local products with local features at local prices; and a bottom-of-the-pyramid segment, as Michigan University's C. K. Prahalad calls it, that can afford to buy only the most inexpensive products. (See C. K. Prahalad and Allen Hammond's "Serving the World's Poor, Profitably," HBR September 2002.) The markets for talent and capital in developing countries are usually structured along the same lines, as we explain in the exhibit "The Four-Tiered Structure of Markets."

Because of the institutional voids in developing countries, multinational companies find it difficult to serve anything but the market's global tier. In product markets, the lack of market research makes it tough for multinational companies to understand customers' tastes, and the paucity of distribution networks makes it

---

The Four-Tiered Structure of Markets

In developing countries, the markets for finished goods (products) and raw materials (factors of production) can be broken up into four distinct components.

At the apex of the market pyramid is the **global tier**. In the product market, this section consists of consumers who want offerings to have the same attributes and quality that products in developed countries have and are willing to pay global prices for them. In the talent market, this tier consists of top-notch managers, such as newly minted graduates from the Indian Institutes of Management, who demand global-level salaries.

Immediately below that is the **glocal tier**. In the product market, this tier consists of consumers who demand customized products of near-global standard and are willing to pay a shade less than global consumers do. An example would be Chinese and Indian executives who prefer to stay in a Shangri-La or Taj hotel rather than at a Four Seasons. In the talent market, this section consists of high-quality managers who will work only for local companies even if the pay is a little less than it would be at multinational corporations.

Consumers in the **local tier** are happy with products of local quality and at local prices. In the talent market, managers in this section will put up with less-than-world-class working conditions as long as they are paid higher-than-average salaries.

The **bottom** of the market consists of people who can afford only the least expensive products.

Multinational corporations typically compete for consumers and talent only in the global tier. Meanwhile, smart local companies, which dominate the local tier, move into the glocal tier and also create breakthrough products for the bottom segment as economies liberalize. These businesses often become emerging giants.

impossible for them to deliver products to customers in the hinterland. In talent markets, they don't have enough knowledge about the local talent pool to design policies that will attract and motivate employees at the glocal, local, and bottom-of-pyramid tiers. Therefore, when a developing country opens up, multinational companies rush into the global tier, and local companies dominate the local tier. There are immense opportunities in the bottom tier, but companies have to use radically different strategies to crack it open. Over time, the glocal tier becomes the battleground between local and foreign corporations. Since glocal customers demand global products with local features, several emerging-market companies have used their knowledge of local markets to serve customers better than multinational firms have been able to, as we shall see in the following pages.

Companies' successes depend on their ability to exploit their competitive advantages. Since emerging giants both circumvent institutional voids and tailor their strategies to local markets better than multinational companies do, they initially take on foreign competitors by capitalizing on their ability to navigate their home turf. They do that by using one of three strategies.

Exploit Understanding of Product Markets

Many emerging-market companies have become world-class businesses by capitalizing on their knowledge of local product markets. They've kept multinational rivals at bay by judiciously adapting to the special characteristics of customers and business ecosystems at home. These emerging giants have also exploited similarities between geographically proximate developing markets to grow across borders.

Product markets often turn out to be unique because customers' needs and tastes are idiosyncratic. Local companies are the first to realize that and to build businesses around distinctive national characteristics. For instance, Jollibee Foods thrives because it realizes that Filipinos like their burgers to have a particular soy and garlic taste; Nandos is growing in South Africa by providing cooked chicken that suits local palates; and Pollo Campero is doing the same in Guatemala. Over the past ten years, these companies have profitably battled American giants like McDonald's and KFC. They have also used their understanding of local preferences to cater to the tastes of the diaspora from their home markets. Jollibee serves Filipino communities in Hong Kong, the Middle East, and California; Nandos has expanded into the United Kingdom and Malaysia; and Pollo Campero sells to Latino communities in Ecuador, El Salvador, Honduras, Mexico, Nicaragua, and Peru, as well as parts of the United States.

Haier became a leader in China's white goods market, in the teeth of competition from GE, Electrolux, and Whirlpool, mainly because it was able to develop products tailored to the needs of Chinese consumers. For example, when Haier discovered that customers in rural China were using the company's washing machines to clean vegetables like sweet potatoes, the company modified its product designs to accommodate that need. The humid weather in Chinese cities such as Shanghai and Shenzhen requires people to change clothes frequently, so Haier created a tiny washing machine that cleans a single set of clothes. Because the model uses less electricity and water than a regular washing machine does, it has become an instant hit in China's coastal cities.

Haier's strategy compels the company to manufacture a large variety of products, but the company exploits its expert knowledge of the Chinese market—knowledge that is hard for multinational companies to obtain—by developing a product for every need.

Haier has also painstakingly created a distribution and service network that covers not only urban markets on the east coast of China but also markets in semi-urban and rural China. In a country where reliable after-sales service and national distribution aren't common, Haier's investments in those two areas have yielded formidable sources of competitive advantage. Product markets often turn out to be hard to penetrate because companies need specialized infrastructures, distribution channels, or delivery systems to meet customers' needs. Most multinational companies, we find, are ill equipped to pioneer the development of such systems.

Interestingly, Haier took care to cement its leadership at home before venturing abroad. By 1991, the company had become China's biggest manufacturer of refrigerators, but it wasn't until 1995 that Haier set up its first joint venture, in Indonesia. It then quickly moved into the Philippines, Malaysia, and Yugoslavia over the next two years. Germany became the first Western market for Haier-branded refrigerators in 1997, and two years later, Haier entered the United States, setting up a design center in Boston, a marketing operation in New York, and a manufacturing facility in South Carolina. In the U.S. market, the Chinese giant has focused on entering price-sensitive segments and on learning how to establish partnerships with American retailers such as Best Buy, Home Depot, and Wal-Mart. In 2005, research firm Euromonitor International reported that Haier had a

26% share of the U.S. market for compact refrigerators (the kind found in college dormitories and hotel rooms) and a 50% share of the market for low-end wine cellars. Haier's ability to develop products for small segments has stood it in good stead overseas: In July 2006, Wal-Mart's Web site listed 59 Haier products, many aimed at college students.

Haier's travels epitomize the globalization journey that emerging giants make when they embrace opportunities in product markets. They instinctively turn to other emerging markets when they initially venture abroad because they have the capabilities to respond to opportunities in such countries. Because of their knowledge of products and cost bases, however, they aren't content with operating only in developing countries. When they enter advanced markets, they tend to avoid head-to-head competition with foreign companies; they focus on niche opportunities that allow them to capitalize on their existing strengths. This approach helps emerging giants gradually stretch their capabilities even as they learn how to operate in developed markets. The experience helps them enlarge their footprints in advanced countries and compete more effectively with multinational giants when their home markets mature. For instance, Haier's experience in Europe and the United States will benefit the company as Western retailers such as Carrefour and Wal-Mart become important distribution channels in China.

Build on Familiarity with Resource Markets

Some emerging-market companies have gained competitive advantage by exploiting their knowledge about local factors of production—the markets for talent and capital—thereby serving customers both at home and abroad in a cost-effective manner.

Consider Indian information technology majors such as Tata Consultancy Services, Infosys Technologies, Wipro, and Satyam Computer Services, all of which have excelled in recent years at catering to the global demand for software and services. This is partly because India's education system produces many engineers and technical graduates; local companies hire these people at salaries much lower than those that engineers in developed markets earn. Since institutional voids pervade the talent market in India, however, it is very difficult for foreign companies to capitalize on the same human resources. Multinational software service providers, such as Accenture and EDS, have a hard time sorting talent in a market where the level of people's skills and the quality of educational institutions vary wildly. In fact, as talent becomes scarcer in urban centers like Bangalore and Delhi, Indian companies will maintain their advantage, because they know how to lure people from India's second-tier cities better than multinational companies do.

Transnational giants also find it tough to operate in an economy with a poor physical infrastructure and to cope with the Indian regulatory apparatus. India's software companies recognized the possibility of providing services to overseas customers at least a decade before Western companies acknowledged the feasibility of hiring Indian software professionals. Consequently, the Indian firms gained experience early, which has kept them ahead of their foreign rivals. Recently, some Indian companies have also been able to tap the global capital and talent markets, nullifying more of their overseas rivals' inherent advantages.

Some companies have exploited their knowledge of local factors of production and supply chains to build world-class businesses. Taiwan-based Inventec, for instance, is among the world's largest manufacturers of notebook computers, PCs, and servers, many of which it makes in China and supplies to Hewlett-Packard and Toshiba. It also makes cellular telephones and portable music players for other multinational companies. Inventec's customers benefit from the low costs of manufacturing products in China without having to invest in factories there. They are also able to use China's talented software and hardware professionals, who can design products quickly in an industry where product life cycles are notoriously short. Inventec has mastered the challenges associated with sourcing electronic omponents from around the world, assembling them into quality products at a low cost, and shipping them to multinational companies in a reliable fashion. Recently, Inventec started selling computers in Taiwan and China under its own brand name. The computers have a Chinese operating system and software, so Inventec doesn't compete directly with its customers—yet.

Likewise, Bunge, the world's largest processor of oilseeds, has created a supply chain that links Brazil's farmers to consumers all over the world. Bunge's savvy trading organization tracks the supply of and demand for oilseeds, which lets executives decide when to buy oilseeds; when and where to crush them; and when and where to transport oil and oil meal for consumer, agricultural, and industrial use. Bunge charters approximately 100 ships; it leases warehouses and crushing plants all over the world; and it even takes equity positions in ports. That infrastructure allows the company to respond quickly to changes in customer requirements and helps it cope with logistics problems, such as those caused by

Hurricane Katrina in 2005. Finally, the $24 billion company feeds supply and demand data to Brazil's farmers, along with advice about everything from fertilizers to harvesting techniques, so they can plant the most profitable kinds of oilseeds. Bunge's sales grew by 235% between 1997 and 2004, from $7.4 billion to $25.1 billion. Its net income has risen by about 425% over the same period, from $83 million to $469 million.

Businesses that are built around raw materials are usually global from their inception, either because they serve customers in advanced markets or because they are part of a global value chain. As they grow, these emerging giants expand their footprints in three ways. First, they look for customers in advanced markets that they can serve from their home bases. Second, as factor markets at home become saturated and thus more expensive, these businesses look for other developing countries that offer similar resources. Finally, these companies move up the value chain, selling branded products or offering solutions to niche segments. That's exactly what India's information technology leaders are doing. After establishing themselves as reliable providers of IT services in North America, they moved into Latin America and Asia. By setting up operations in developing countries such as China and Russia, they have started exploiting the large pools of talent in those countries. They have also acquired small consulting firms in the United States and Europe, thereby enhancing their ability to develop high-end solutions for customers.

Treat Institutional Voids as Business Opportunities

The third way to build emerging giants is for private sector businesses to fill institutional voids. Only governments can set up certain institutions, but companies can own and profitably operate many kinds of intermediaries in product and factor markets.

Many institutional intermediaries facilitate the flow of information in markets; these include newspaper publishers and database vendors. Some intermediaries enhance the credibility of the claims sellers make—for instance, accounting firms, quality-certification firms, and accreditation agencies. Others analyze information and advise buyers and sellers; these include rating agencies, product-rating companies such as JD Power and Associates, and publications that rank universities and professional schools. Private sector institutions can also facilitate transactions, either by aggregating and distributing goods and services or by creating forums where buyers and sellers can conduct their own transactions. The aggregators—venture capitalists, private-equity firms, and banks in the financial market; retailers in the product market; and, to some extent, universities in the talent market—help buyers and sellers find each other. Stock exchanges, online auction sites, and job sites on the Internet serve as forums where transactions can take place in the financial, product, and talent markets, respectively. (For more on two-sided markets, see Thomas Eisenmann, Geoffrey Parker, and Marshall W. Van Alstyne's "Strategies for Two-Sided Markets," HBR October 2006.)

Multinational companies enjoy an edge in the intermediaries business because they bring expertise, credibility, and experience to the table. However, emerging-market companies can take them on for three reasons. First, many intermediaries are people intensive, so running them requires familiarity with the local language and culture. Second, intermediaries are information intensive, and it takes local expertise to access scattered information and analyze data of variable quality. Third, governments consider some institutions, such as media, banking, and financial services, to be of national importance. They often prohibit multinational companies from setting up those institutions or force them to collaborate with local companies.

Resource markets can be separated into the four tiers we discussed earlier—one global and three local. Multinational companies are suited to serve as intermediaries in the global tier, but local firms are better able to cater to the other tiers. For example, multinational banks serve large blue-chip customers in emerging markets because evaluating those companies' creditworthiness is relatively straightforward. Those businesses produce high-quality financial statements, get them audited by globally reputable accountants, and, if their shares are listed overseas, follow international accounting norms. However, evaluating the credit of small and medium enterprises is tough: There's so little data on them. Domestic banks, with their local knowledge and informal connections, cater to this segment better than foreign banks do. In Turkey, for example, the likes of Citibank skim the top of the corporate market whereas local banks, like Garanti Bank Turkey and Akbank, cater to Turkish businesses better than the multinational banks do.

Several emerging giants have learned to play the role of market institutions. Consider Old Mutual, an insurance company that realized that South Africa lacked mutual funds and other long-term investment products. Old Mutual responded by creating insurance policies for poor people that had the features of savings accounts. By marketing the policies to millions of South Africans, the company became a large financial services firm. When the South African economy integrated itself with the world market in the early 1990s, Old Mutual moved into other African countries, such as Botswana, Kenya, Malawi, Namibia, and Zimbabwe, and listed itself on the Johannesburg and London stock exchanges.

To take another example, Agora is one of Poland's most successful media companies. It publishes Poland's biggest newspaper, *Gazeta Wyborcza* (GW), which commands 43% of the national readership and has a 62% share of national newspaper advertising revenues. The paper started in April 1989 as an organ for the Solidarity political movement, but after Solidarity's victory in Poland's elections in June 1989, Agora's founders made the newspaper an independent organization. Agora filled the information void in Poland by providing not only news coverage but also a vehicle for advertising. Since GW's readers are educated, live in urban areas, and have plenty of disposable income, the newspaper's advertisers include travel agencies, automakers, cellular phone companies, pension funds, and so on. The company trades on the Warsaw and London stock exchanges, which has enabled it to raise capital to fund its growth. In 1993, the company sold approximately 20% of its shares to Cox Enterprises, an American media company. The alliance enabled Agora to get expertise and capital from Cox.

China's Emerge Logistics is another company that has exploited an institutional void in an emerging market to create a profitable business. Although China has plenty of eight-lane highways, delivering goods isn't easy because the transportation system is underdeveloped. No trucking firm operates nationally; in fact, the average Chinese trucking company owns only one or two vehicles. In addition, separate government bodies regulate air, rail, road, and river transport, and several levels of government impose tolls on vehicles. These factors add to companies' costs and hinder them from distributing products. Emerge Logistics, one of China's few third-party logistics services providers, helps multi-national companies sell products all over the country by capitalizing on its understanding of the disjointed transportation system and the baffling bureaucracy. Operating from a warehouse an hour away from Shanghai, Emerge Logistics takes foreign companies all the way through the delivery process—from filing import applications before goods enter the country to collecting payments from customers. The company coordinates the transfer of goods among different modes of transportation and takes orders from Chinese customers for its clients' products. By doing the billing itself, Emerge Logistics also facilitates direct sales by Western multinational companies to Chinese customers.

Exploiting institutional opportunities often doesn't create a launchpad for globalization. That doesn't mean these businesses stay small, however. In markets such as Brazil, China, India, and Russia, institutional businesses can become quite large even if they focus only on the domestic market. In smaller emerging markets, companies that try to fill institutional voids can grow by exploiting adjacent opportunities. A print media company, for instance, can expand into electronic media; a bank can diversify into asset management and investment banking; and a privately owned business school can set up a medical, law, or technology school. Doing so often paves the way for these businesses to go global at a later stage.

The Importance of Execution and Governance

Identifying the right growth strategy is critical for building a world-class business, but execution and governance determine whether companies in emerging markets can realize their potential. While that may be true about building great companies anywhere, our research suggests that excellent execution and good governance are particularly valuable in newly industrializing countries. Financial and talent resources in emerging markets are scarce, but companies that can execute well end up getting more out of them. And since resource providers cannot rely on the enforcement of contracts in emerging markets, good governance—organizational mechanisms that ensure that a company lives up to its commitments to investors, customers, employees, and business partners—allows an organization to acquire a reputation that is invaluable in its dealings with constituents. It can, for instance, access the best resources at the lowest cost.

The manner in which emerging-market companies achieve good governance varies greatly. Countries put different weights on the extent to which a governance system should protect shareholders, employees, and other constituents. The laws regarding corporate governance differ across nations, with greater similarities among those that share economic links such as trading connections. Governance practices vary even more. However, only companies that zealously protect the interests of shareholders and employees, and ensure that both receive competitive returns on investment, become emerging giants.

Is it better to be more global? The answer may appear to be yes. Well-managed companies do spread their wings over time and enter many geographic markets. There is a correlation between global scope and performance. But executives shouldn't confuse that with a causal relationship. What is important is whether global scope results in competitive advantage rather than being the result of advantage derived in some other fashion. Our research shows that there's more than one way to skin the proverbial cat: Some emerging giants operate in several countries, but others sell only at home. In fact, look at the United Nations Conference on Trade and Development's list of top 50 emerging-market companies, and you'll see that the correlation between size and degree of globalization in these businesses (as measured by market value) is, at 0.4, low. Moreover, the financial performance of world-class companies that have diversified across countries isn't superior to the performance of those that haven't. Emerging giants can thus be successful even if they don't have global footprints.

Originally published in October 2006
Reprint R0610C

Inside the Mind
of the Chinese Consumer

WILLIAM MCEWEN, XIAOGUANG FANG,

CHUANPING ZHANG, AND

RICHARD BURKHOLDER

Executive Summary

FOR THE PAST THREE DECADES, the torrid pace of
GDP growth in China has fascinated companies around
the world. Western companies, in particular, have
viewed the Middle Kingdom as a production powerhouse, a multinational marketer's dream come true, or an
increasingly capable competitor in branded goods marketing. But are those views grounded in reality?

To find out, the Gallup Organization undertook an
ambitious ten-year, nationwide survey of Chinese consumers and employees. The group found that many of
the perceptions held by companies outside—and even
inside—China are inaccurate. Specifically, the findings
belie at least four commonly held notions. The first is that
the Chinese people, unmoored from collectivism, are
now focused chiefly on working hard and getting rich.
The second is that the Chinese workers now flooding the
factories and offices of large cities are highly ambitious

and actively engaged. The third is that the new prosperity in China allows consumers there to buy much of what they want. And the fourth is that there remains an endless hunger for household basics.

Indeed, the survey found that most Chinese citizens are more interested in expressing their individuality than in getting rich. It also showed that Chinese workers are not as engaged by their jobs as the world might think. What's more, with the average citizen making less than $1,800 per year, only the affluent have extra money to spend. Finally, the average Chinese consumer is more interested in buying luxury and entertainment items than in purchasing basic household goods.

The Gallup survey provides much-needed scope and depth of hard data documenting the Chinese consumer—giving policy makers and executives the tools to manage the opportunities and challenges in China.

Ever since china began to emerge from its Maoist cocoon by welcoming foreign investment, the torrid pace of GDP growth in the Middle Kingdom has been fascinating companies around the globe. During the past ten years, that fascination has increased, giving rise to unclear and even conflicting ideas about what it means to do business in or with China.

Western companies, in particular, have tended to view China as a potent production powerhouse, a multinational marketer's dream come true, or an increasingly capable competitor in branded goods marketing. Many of them see China as the world's largest factory. This belief is understandable, since the country now turns out a remarkable range of products, from clothing to toys to computer components. And the production capacity may be limitless, as the country appears to be blessed with a seemingly inexhaustible reservoir of cheap labor.

Another common notion is that China is a consumer giant keen to slake its thirst with products of all kinds. Some see an eager business-to-business customer, ready to buy increasingly vast quantities of raw materials from countries such as Australia, Russia, and Brazil in order to stoke its production furnaces. Others focus more on the business-to-consumer opportunities—the fantasy of getting a billion consumers to buy previously unavailable foreign goods ranging from shampoo to luxury automobiles. Taken together, these hopes and beliefs have long spurred business press articles, workshops, "Webinars," and corporate investments. Yet without a reliable portrait of who the Chinese people are or how they're changing, corporate planners have struggled to define and address the apparent opportunities afforded by the world's most populous nation. In the absence of solid data about China and its people, myth and conjecture have prevailed.

To fill this information void, we at the Gallup Organization undertook an ambitious ten-year, nationwide survey of the Chinese people, beginning in 1994 and ending in 2004. Unlike other surveys, the Gallup effort looked at the habits, hopes, and plans of all Chinese adults, from rural farmers to city dwellers. Following the baseline survey in 1994, Gallup completed three additional countrywide surveys, each garnering more than 3,000 responses. Our goal was to discover what the people of China really want. The data culled from the surveys represent not just a snapshot but a moving picture of the Chinese people's changing tastes and desires during a decade of explosive development.

The data suggest that many of the perceptions held by companies outside—and even inside—China are inaccurate. Specifically, our findings belie at least four commonly held notions. The first misconception is that the Chinese people, unmoored from collectivism, are now focused chiefly on working hard and getting rich. The second is that the Chinese workers now flooding the factories and offices of the large cities are highly ambitious, fully mobilized, and actively engaged. The third is that the new prosperity in China allows consumers there to buy much of what they want. And the fourth is that there remains an endless hunger for household basics.

Gallup sought to document the activities, aspirations, and intentions of the Chinese consumer—and to provide corporate planners, marketers, employers, and policy makers with the tools they need to manage the opportunities and challenges in China. Armed with this information, companies can begin to correct the misconceptions and formulate a more grounded approach to doing business in and with China.

The Chinese Work Ethic

The impressive output of Chinese factories seems like a formidable challenge to countries and companies hoping to compete. But current output is no guarantee of future output. It's important to ask, How strong is the work ethic of Chinese laborers today, and how closely does their current productivity match up to their imagined potential?

Our surveys examined the Chinese work ethic through a series of questions addressing the personal philosophies of workers. We asked about their fundamental attitudes toward work and what's really important to them. We wanted to know what people are seeking from life and how their jobs fit with their ambitions. We also sought to learn about work environments—how conducive they are to productivity and how well managed they are. Our findings seem to contradict many popular assumptions about China's workforce.

Misconception 1: The primary aim of Chinese workers is to work hard and get rich. We found that few Chinese workers adhere to a self-effacing, stereotypically collectivist "give in service to society" attitude toward work; only 2% of respondents held that view in 2004, down from 4% in 1994. Given the increasing openness of Chinese markets and citizens' apparent embrace of entrepreneurial opportunities, this is not surprising. What is surprising is that the number of respondents who adopted a seemingly more capitalistic view ("work hard and get rich") dropped far more significantly, by 15 percentage points between 1994 and 2004. (See the exhibit "Whither Personal Ambition?")

Rather, what has grown, in lockstep with the country's economic surge and its rising standard of living, has been the proportion of people saying that their personal goals are self-satisfaction and self-expression. Instead of worrying about the taste (or availability) of the next meal, the increasingly affluent Chinese worker is thinking about the taste of life itself. The percentage of Chinese exhibiting this feeling has more than doubled in a decade. Self-satisfaction is now the number one motivator in the big cities of Beijing, Guangzhou, and Shanghai; it is the principal objective among the young, edging out "work hard and get rich" among 18- to 24-year-olds. It has also become the predominant aspiration among the most affluent.

The data suggest that we're witnessing the emergence of a Chinese "me" generation. But individual motivation is merely one portion of the productivity puzzle. How that motivation is guided and harnessed in pursuit of company objectives is a management issue. Here, too, the surveys reveal important news.

Misconception 2: Chinese workers are highly dedicated. For years, companies outside China have viewed its workforce as impressively eager to churn out never-ending streams of lower-cost products for any firm smart enough to relocate its production operations there. No doubt, the number of workers is enormous. But ambition and eagerness are another matter entirely.

For some years, Gallup has been asking a standard set of 12 questions to assess the emotional bonds between workers and their companies. (For more on these measures, see John H. Fleming, Curt Coffman, and James K. Harter's article "Manage Your Human Sigma," HBR July–August 2005.) This employee-engagement metric

---

Whither Personal Ambition?

While working hard and getting rich are certainly priorities for most Chinese, our survey shows that over the last ten years, these aims have become less important to the average citizen. Instead, Chinese workers are demonstrating an increasing desire to express their individuality— a trend that may just signal the emergence of a new "me" generation.

Closest to own attitude:	1994	2004
"Work hard and get rich."	68%	53%
"Don't think of money/fame; live a life that suits my own tastes."	10%	26%
"Never think of self; give in service to society."	4%	2%

has been used to gauge the strength of employee-to-company relationships for a single company, an industry, or across an entire country. In 2004, these questions were used in a onetime survey conducted across China, in which Gallup interviewed more than a thousand urban-dwelling workers.

It is important to note that some of the basic requirements for a productive workplace are indeed present in China. Like their counterparts in Germany, Japan, and the United States, Chinese workers know what their jobs require of them. But that isn't enough to ensure a continuously productive workforce. The data show that Chinese workers feel their efforts are insufficiently rewarded and recognized. Though employees are increasingly focused on fulfilling their personal ambitions, relatively few feel that their companies give them important opportunities to learn and develop. (See the exhibit "Living to Work.")

Our 2004 survey found that 68% of employees don't feel engaged[1]; that is, they don't approach their work with passion or feel a personal connection to their jobs. These employees have essentially checked out; they are sleepwalking through their workdays. And a further 20% of employees hate their jobs to the point of active disengagement. They may well act out their unhappiness, undermining what their engaged coworkers accomplish. Our survey also suggests that the larger the organization, the less employees feel personally connected to the workplace.

When 88% of employees aren't interested in their jobs, productivity suffers—even in a mass-production, assembly-line culture—and that loss typically results in greater absenteeism, more on-the-job accidents, and lower overall performance. The quality of China's

products and services may even reflect this reduced productivity. Perhaps this is one reason why consumers in
China's urban centers hold such low opinions of "Made
in China" versus "Made in Germany" or "Made in Japan."

Living to Work

*In 2004, Gallup found that only a small percentage of urban Chinese
employees felt engaged by their work. This lack of enthusiasm may signal
productivity problems.*

	% of urban Chinese workers who strongly agree:
I know what is expected of me at work	34%
I have the materials and equipment I need to do my work right	32%
At work, I have the opportunity to do what I do best every day	26%
In the last seven days, I have received recognition or praise for doing good work	12%
My supervisor, or someone at work, seems to care about me as a person	26%
Someone at work encourages my development	23%
At work, my opinions seem to count	20%
The mission or purpose of my company makes me feel my job is important	30%
My associates or fellow employees are committed to doing quality work	27%
I have a best friend at work	43%
In the last six months, someone at work has talked to me about my progress	19%
This last year, I have had opportunities at work to learn and grow	23%

(See "Made in China, for China" at the end of this article.) Indeed, the engagement profiles of Chinese workers stand in sharp contrast to those of workers in many countries China competes with. For example, Gallup's U.S. employee-engagement database (as of 2004) shows that 29% of workers are engaged, while 16% are actively disengaged. The ratio of engaged to actively disengaged flips in China, where the actively disengaged greatly outnumber the engaged.

The management challenge. Clearly, Chinese management practice has lagged behind the changes in employee attitudes. If our 2004 survey accurately reflects worker attitudes, it could be that Chinese managers are still acting as if their reports were automatons rather than human beings with individual strengths, needs, and growth potential. The lack of focus on human development may also contribute to the continuing shortage of leadership talent among domestic and multinational companies operating in China.

Certainly, China can continue to churn out goods, since the countryside is still filled with young Chinese eager to earn a living. But without engaged workers, it appears that China's true performance potential will not be realized. Any factory that experiences a 22% drop in a "work hard" philosophy (see the exhibit "Whither Personal Ambition?") is one where management must search for more creative ways to stoke the furnaces and stimulate the assembly line.

By and large, it seems that China's famed work ethic is not what it appears to be; perhaps it never was. Given China's culture and history—as well as its focus on high-production operations—Chinese managers may not embrace the idea that an efficient assembly line requires personal gratification and individual development. But if

Chinese factories are to compete with companies like Toyota, Mars, or Stryker, these issues must be addressed.

Many experts have said that the opportunities now afforded by China's entrance into the World Trade Organization will open the door for marketing-savvy and smartly managed multinationals. With an increasing number of Western multinationals managing factories in China, different HR policies, practices, and people management methods will no doubt be introduced. Of course, not all Western companies employ enlightened and worker-focused management practices; and given the cultural differences between East and West, there's no guarantee that Western management methods will provide a better fit with the needs and hopes of Chinese workers.

Still, savvy and creatively managed outsider companies will want to take note of the important evolution, if not revolution, in workers' feelings about what they desire and expect from life and work. Firms such as Procter & Gamble, Starbucks, GM (Buick), and KFC have made inroads into China partly because they've correctly anticipated emerging consumer needs; in the long term, however, their success depends on the active assistance of their employees. The trainloads of rural workers arriving in the cities require human resource management and skill development. Until that happens, the output potential of the Chinese factory remains merely that: potential.

Beyond the Basics

The Gallup surveys also set out to discover what the Chinese consumer is eager to buy. As a country of 1.3 billion people with, as the cliché goes, 2.6 billion armpits to deodorize, China has always appealed to the pecuniary imaginations of Western marketers. The size of the prize has been so tempting as to encourage steep company investments, even in the absence of solid evidence about consumer demand.

Misconception 3: Chinese consumers now have a lot of money to spend. Certainly, the endless drumbeat in the media about China's increasing prosperity supports the image of a growing high-potential market—but a market isn't about size alone. Consumers must not only want to buy products but also have the money to do so. While Chinese buyers are many, and incomes are rising, most citizens remain too poor to purchase what they want. Despite the overall increase in household income— the average income rose 30% from 1997 to 2004—China's average household income in 2004 was still less than $1,800. What's more, only 5% of Chinese now say they're "very satisfied" with their household incomes—a drop from 9% in 2000. In fact, the average Chinese citizen is more likely to express dissatisfaction than satisfaction, with one in five "very dissatisfied" with current earnings.

Even the relatively affluent, while clearly happier about their income status, are hardly complacent. Only 7% of the highest earners say they're "very satisfied" with their incomes, and more than one in four upper-income Chinese say they're to some degree dissatisfied.

Misconception 4: The biggest markets among Chinese consumers are for basic household products. We learned a decade ago that only 6% of Chinese households owned a vacuum cleaner and 25% owned a refrigerator. Given those numbers, it would seem logical that, with their rising incomes, more Chinese consumers would want these items. Certainly, the average Chinese household is now much more likely to have a TV set, a phone, a refrigerator, a vacuum cleaner, and a washing machine than it was a decade ago. But the rate at which these products are now purchased pales compared with that of higher-technology products—products that may not save labor but rather enhance enjoyment and entertainment that satisfies individual tastes. Within a decade, ownership of color TVs increased by almost half. The percentage of households reporting they have DVD players jumped from 7% in 1997 to 52% in 2004. The number of households with computers grew from 2% in 1994 to 13% in 2004, and the number of those with mobile phones jumped from 10% in 1999 to 48% in 2004.

What does all this mean for a company planning to do business in China? First, it's clear that aspirations are growing, that desire is outstripping ability, and that the traditional bellwethers of modernization don't necessarily apply. Chinese consumers want more than just function. This is one reason why Nokia, which has emphasized fashion over function, has seen its cell phone sales in China rocket past those of Motorola and Ericsson. If a company wants to sell vacuums or washing machines in China, it had better pay attention to emotional needs as well as physical ones. And if it's selling microwave ovens, air conditioners, and TVs, it should be sure those products are as fashionable as they are reliable.

The ripe urban market. Some Western managers see the continuing rise in China's average income as an opportunity across an entire nation. Others divide China into two worlds: the cities of Beijing, Guangzhou, and Shanghai; and all other locations. Both perspectives are incomplete. While it's true that average income has increased, some Chinese are benefiting far more than others. And while there are sharp differences between the incomes of urban and rural dwellers (urban Chinese earn almost three times more than rural dwellers do), affluence is growing not just in the big three cities but in what has been termed the "third China"—the midsize cities such as Xi'an, Nanjing, and Wuhan, which may afford some of the largest opportunities for marketers.

Indeed, a relatively well-to-do segment is expanding briskly across the nation. In 1997, about 3.5% of Chinese households had annual incomes of 30,000 renminbi (about $3,800). In just five years, that figure skyrocketed to over 12%; half of those living in the big three cities have achieved this level of income. These consumers can afford the products that other Chinese may only dream about.

In some product categories, where consumers live appears to be a more important predictor of spending than affluence. This may reflect the needs of urban dwellers for products such as air conditioners or the availability of technology support for items such as computers. In other categories, like automobiles, affluence is the largest predictor of ownership.

By and large, affluent urban dwellers already own a fair amount of what they want: Televisions and mobile phones are ubiquitous. Accordingly, opportunities in this market spring more from upgrades than from first-time product sales. The product-marketing game in the affluent world is now about brand share. Though marketers will still use the first-time-sale approach in rural areas, many affluent city dwellers will now be drawing on their direct experiences and will be persuaded not only by company-managed communications but, more powerfully, by word of mouth.

Look Out for Generation Y

Companies should forget what they've learned about China's Generation X—people currently in their late twenties and thirties—when marketing to the country's late teens and early twentysomethings, or Generation Y. They should also forget what they've learned about Generation Y in Germany, the United States, or Brazil, where this age group is often viewed as a generation of slackers. China's Generation Y has increasing drive, hopes, and demands; it is a highly literate and information-savvy group that refuses to be taken for granted. These young adults are open to Western ideas and products, yet still proudly supportive of their own culture. And they're apparently on a buying spree.

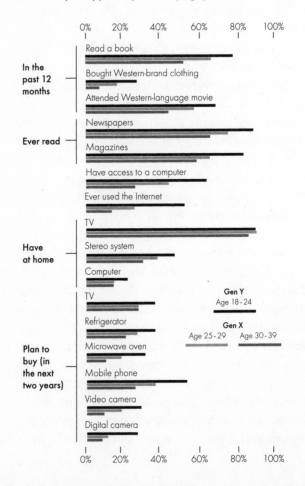

The survey data also reveal important differences among products segments. Not all are growing equally; some appear to be quickly gaining appeal, while others are merely edging forward—or even backsliding. Overall, the Chinese appetite continues to be strong for certain must-have items, including TVs and mobile phones, hard goods such as refrigerators and air conditioners, and "fun" products such as stereos and digital cameras (computers and video cameras are just heating up).

Importantly, the speed of development in China is such that new technologies may well replace old ones before the older ones even have a chance to get established. For example, we're seeing the digital camera rocket past the film camera, the VCD zoom past the VCR, and the mobile phone bypass the landline. In fact, more than 80% of all city dwellers own a mobile phone, and 33% of these people say they're planning to buy another one.

The automobile is an exception—it is still poised for first purchases. As of 2004, only 10% of those in the highest income bracket owned a car. Though intense competition is forcing prices to drop, cars still cost two to three times most people's annual income. Even so, appreciable numbers of consumers are actively planning to acquire one. It's small wonder that companies like GM, Volkswagen, and DaimlerChrysler continue to have strong interest in China. With an estimated upside of 100 million to 130 million potential buyers, even a small market share translates to an impressively large number of units sold. If only 2% of this total estimated market were to buy cars in the next two years, that would still be an increase of about 39% over the current level of car sales there. What's more, this 2% would represent a whopping 22% of GM's total worldwide sales in 2004. (See the exhibit "What Urban and Affluent Chinese Consumers Want [2004].")

For the time being, marketers in China will find their biggest consumers among the urban and the affluent. And "affluent" no longer means just the top 3% to 5% of Chinese consumers; the wealthy class is growing, so creative-financing options may be the way to attract this group. Conspicuous consumption is as apparent in the Middle Kingdom as it is in the West, and lots of attention is being paid to staying current.

OUR SURVEYS INDICATE that the Chinese consumer is indeed clamoring for a great many goods and services.

What Urban and Affluent Chinese Consumers Want (2004)

Some of the most sought-after products in China are TVs, mobile phones, computers, and digital cameras.

Plan to buy in the next two years:	Among those living in the big three cities (Beijing, Guangzhou, and Shanghai)	Among those making 30,000 renminbi or more a year
TV	27%	34%
Refrigerator	21%	24%
Air conditioner	23%	26%
Microwave oven	17%	23%
Stereo system	20%	23%
DVD/VCD player	18%	16%
Mobile phone	34%	15%
Computer	28%	31%
Digital camera	29%	29%
Automobile	13%	16%

But this hunger doesn't necessarily mirror that seen in other countries. What sells in Turkey or Chile or Thailand may not be what sells in China. China is in many ways unlike any other developing market. The Chinese consumer is neither complacent nor compliant, and rapid change is now the norm. In China, the past may be a poor predictor of the future. So captains of industry must ask themselves, Are we poised to capitalize on the real growth opportunities?

Despite the many thousands of years of Chinese history, China's longest journey in some ways has only just begun. We are witnessing not only the dawn of a new millennium there but a new era in which the emotions, attitudes, and perceptions of the man and woman on the street, in the home, and in the factory increasingly matter.

Made in China, for China

HOW WELL ARE CHINESE COMPANIES doing in meeting the needs and desires of their country's people? On one hand, the powerful domestic behemoths such as appliance maker Haier and computer giant Lenovo seem to be entrenched in the marketplace. Companies like these have also been setting up operations abroad, seeking to acquire companies such as Maytag and Thomson and divisions such as IBM's PC business, and announcing their ambitious worldwide goals. But are Chinese consumers really devoted to Chinese brands?

Our ten-year research (1994 to 2004) shows that a "Made in China" label doesn't guarantee protection against newer, more exciting, and perhaps more relevant foreign competitors. Despite the fact that almost two-thirds of Chinese say they prefer to buy durable goods or major appliances made in China (and only one-fifth feel that way about products made in other countries), our surveys also show that consumers are increasingly concerned about the quality of domestic products. Our 2004 survey found that only 21% of Chinese consumers feel that the quality of the country's durable products is very good, while even fewer (8%) feel it is excellent, 37% feel it is fair, and 3% think it's poor.

Consumers' preference for domestic goods has dropped from 78% to 67% in the last five years, and it's a good deal lower—and declining faster—among the young, the affluent, and the urban. At the same time, preference for foreign goods, perhaps most notably European brands, has risen from 19% to 22%.

While most Chinese consumers haven't stated a clear preference for foreign goods over those produced in China, they are aware that they now have options. For example, in home electronics (particularly TV sets), our surveys show that most Chinese consumers are aware of Changhong (87%) and Haier (83%), but most are also aware of Panasonic (74%), Philips (70%), and Samsung (70%).

Global competition in China is perhaps most obvious in automobiles, where a wide variety of international brands are already well known, including the once-dominant market leader Volkswagen as well as domestic makers such as Chery and Shanghai Automotive and foreign marques such as Buick, Toyota, Mercedes, and BMW.

Chinese consumers' hesitancy about goods made at home may or may not be grounded in product performance. And product performance may or may not be linked to issues of employee engagement. Regardless, if Chinese companies are to fully realize their opportunities in New York and Paris, they must make certain that their products are selling well in China. After all, not all ambitious export initiatives are successful. Some are Hondas, but some are Yugos.

Notes

1. Gallup established three categories of workers—"engaged," "not engaged," and "actively disengaged"—on the basis of responses to the 12 queries listed in the exhibit "Living to Work." Sixty-eight percent is the proportion of Chinese workers in 2004 who were not engaged.

Originally published in March 2006
Reprint R0603D

Cocreating Business's New Social Compact

JEB BRUGMANN AND C. K. PRAHALAD

Executive Summary

MOVING BEYOND DECADES of mutual distrust and animosity, corporations and nongovernmental organizations (NGOs) are learning to cooperate with each other. Realizing that their interests are converging, the two sides are working together to create innovative business models that are helping to grow new markets and accelerate the eradication of poverty.

The path to convergence has proceeded in three stages. In the initial be-responsible stage, companies and NGOs, realizing that they had to coexist, started to look for ways to influence each other through joint social responsibility projects. This experience paved the way for the get-into-business stage, in which NGOs and companies sought to serve the poor by setting up successful businesses. In the process, NGOs learned business discipline from the private sector, while corporations gained an appreciation for the local knowledge, low-cost business models, and community-based marketing techniques that the NGOs have mastered.

Increased success on both sides has laid the foundation for the cocreate-business stage, in which companies and NGOs become key parts of each other's capacity to deliver value. When BP sought to market a duel-fuel portable stove in India, it set up one such cocreation system with three Indian NGOs. The system allowed BP to bring the innovative stove to a geographically dispersed market through myriad local distributors without incurring distribution costs so high that the product would become unaffordable. The company sold its stoves profitably, the NGOs gained access to a lucrative revenue stream that could fund other projects, and consumers got more than the ability to sit down to a hot meal—they got the opportunity to earn incomes as the local distributors and thus to gain economic and social influence.

IN EARLY 2005, we met privately with the chairperson of one of the world's biggest banks to discuss business opportunities in catering to poor people. The chairperson responded bluntly. "We don't care about making profits [on such a business]," he said, with the bank's CEO sitting beside him. "There's something even distasteful about the idea of making money off people who earn less than $1 a day." He raised a related issue that, unexpectedly, became the topic of our discussion that morning: how the bank could create, manage, and scale up a program to support elementary schools for poor children in a certain developing country. We were a little surprised that a banker was so preoccupied with a problem that usually keeps not-for-profit, nongovernmental organizations (NGOs), rather than large corporations, up at night.

A week later, we spent a day with representatives of three relatively small NGOs in India. One specializes in infrastructure development and postdisaster reconstruction. Another focuses on the cultivation and processing of herbal medicines. The third provides business support to rural enterprises. Together, the three organizations also manage several self-help savings and loan groups involving around 50,000 women. The NGOs and their business advisers, some of them executives working for a large global company, wanted our help in deciding which businesses to set up. They had conducted research and market tests on opportunities in the financial services and insurance, construction, consumer products, and health services industries. By the end of the day, the NGOs decided to go ahead with three businesses: selling insurance products, retailing groceries, and providing sanitation facilities to people whose income is around 50 cents a day. We were impressed by the NGOs' desire and readiness to organize local communities so they could manufacture and sell products in the marketplace—just like good entrepreneurs.

Those two meetings, we're convinced, captured more than a fleeting role reversal; they symbolize an enduring shift in the practices of corporations and social groups and, perhaps, in their attitudes toward each other. That may sound like a startling claim. Since the protests against globalization at Seattle and Davos in the late 1990s, people have assumed that the gulf between the private sector and the civil society, as the media call NGOs, has been growing. After all, despite social groups' protests, more countries have opened up to foreign investment, and governments have continued to privatize industries. Meanwhile, companies, especially Western multinational corporations, have come under a dark cloud. Their recent shenanigans—fraud at Enron, insider trading at WorldCom, and inept governance at Hewlett-Packard, not to mention a rash of social, environmental, and health-related controversies at blue-chip companies such as Nike, Shell, and McDonald's—have led to a near crisis of confidence in the role of the modern corporation in society.

However, a countertrend has emerged. Over the last five years, some corporations have started to pay attention to customers at the bottom of the economic pyramid. As the pioneers move into inner cities and villages, their middle managers are spending more time than you might imagine on acquiring local knowledge, value engineering, developing low-cost business models, and community-based marketing. Meanwhile, several NGOs have set up businesses to provide jobs and incomes in order to free people from the tyranny of poverty. Product development, logistics, project management, and scaling techniques are some of the mechanisms they're using to kickstart socioeconomic development in long-neglected communities.

Realizing that they each possess competencies, infrastructure, and knowledge that the other needs to be able to operate in low-income markets, companies and NGOs are trying to learn from and work with each other. For example, Danone has set up a joint venture with Bangladesh's Grameen Bank to manufacture and sell bottom-of-the-pyramid dairy products. Microsoft has tied up with the NGO Pratham to deliver personal computers to Indian villagers, while Intel and two large Indian information technology firms, Wipro and HCL

Infosystems, have launched the Community PC in partnership with other NGOs to do the same. Nestlé has
joined hands with health professionals and NGOs in
Colombia, Peru, and the Philippines to deliver educational programs on nutrition and nutritionally fortified
food products to the poor.

As their interests and capabilities converge, these corporations and NGOs are together creating innovative
business models that are helping to grow new markets at
the bottom of the pyramid and niche segments in
mature markets. These models, we believe, will lead to
novel frameworks that can renew the corporation's
social legitimacy even as they allow for sustainable development and accelerate the eradication of poverty. This
convergence is making it imperative that managers in
both sectors understand the opportunities and risks in
working together.

Liberalization's Unexpected Consequences

Companies and NGOs have arrived at the same place by
different routes. Over the last two decades, as many
countries opened their economies to foreign competition, often at the behest of the International Monetary
Fund and the World Bank, business and the civil society
fought bitterly. At first, both sides battled vociferously
and publicly with governments over the need for, the
nature of, and the pace of economic reforms. While companies, especially multinational corporations, wanted
governments to reduce tariffs sharply and allow foreign
investment into every sector immediately, the civil society argued that liberalization should take place slowly
and only in some industries. Then, as governments soft-
ened labor, environmental, and investment regulations

to attract foreign investment, the two sectors waged a shadow war over the reforms' future. Finally, as governments played less and less of a regulatory role, corporations and NGOs fought each other directly, debating the boundaries within which socially responsible corporations should operate. Those battles led to three unanticipated consequences.

First, NGOs emerged as the corporate sector's de facto regulators, occupying the vacuum that governments were leaving behind. They aren't newcomers to the task; for many years, NGOs have influenced markets in areas such as chemical regulation, oil spill liability, air emissions, liquid waste, pharmaceutical and food standards, child labor, and employment discrimination. Their influence has created a regulatory framework tougher than the legal requirements corporations face. NGOs may be small, but through the Internet, even a single person or organization can coordinate "smart mobs," as Howard Rheingold calls them in his 2002 book of the same name, allowing NGOs to mount actions on several fronts simultaneously. For instance, local NGOs attacked the Coca-Cola Company over its use of water in the village of Plachimada in Kerala, India. As accounts have spread from Web site to Web site, the dispute has grown into a worldwide battle over the brand's presence in universities and schools. The escalation of the campaign from market to market and from issue to issue has, as the *Wall Street Journal* wrote, cost Coca-Cola "millions of dollars in lost sales and legal fees in India, and growing damage to its reputation elsewhere."

By publicly inflicting harm to a market leader's reputation, which eventually forces the entire industry to change its practices, the civil society is often successful in getting corporations to conform to its norms. For instance, NGOs' attacks on Nike for violating human rights, on Merck and GlaxoSmithKline for enforcing patents on AIDS medicines, and on Monsanto for introducing genetically modified seeds forced the apparel, pharmaceutical, and agribusiness industries to develop new strategies and rewrite their codes of conduct.

Second, companies have invested heavily to develop expertise to cope with NGOs. They have spent time and money launching countercampaigns to protect their reputations. At first, they did so defensively, using social marketing slogans in advertisements and setting up nonprofit entities with which they maintained arm's-length relationships. Over time, they developed more proactive strategies. Smart corporations, for instance, have learned to take their case directly to consumers. They have developed corporate social responsibility (CSR) initiatives, voluntary self-regulation schemes, and cause-based marketing programs. More recently, they have launched public-interest-cum-advertising campaigns, such as Chevron's on global energy issues and Unilever's on women's beauty, self-esteem, and eating disorders. To run such programs, companies have hired people from the social sector who can bring their networks, credibility, and understanding of NGOs into corporations. For instance, Microsoft's director of community affairs worked with NGOs, the World Bank, and a social venture-capital fund for more than 20 years before joining the software giant. Some corporations are even competing with social groups. By launching coffee, tea, and confectionary products with a guarantee that disadvantaged producers are getting a better deal, for example, North American and European manufacturers and retailers are competing with Fairtrade Labelling Organizations International, which enforces its standards on NGOs and member companies.

Third, markets are emerging as an arena in which companies and NGOs interact. Liberalization has provided corporations with access to new consumers, but reaching low-income customers is difficult nonetheless. Executives have to invent new business models if they are to succeed in those markets, and they often find that NGOs possess the knowledge, local infrastructure, and relationships necessary to make them work. There are NGOs that have created large distribution networks that can furnish food, medicine, and credit, especially in remote areas. They have developed a deep understanding of local cultures and consumption habits. And they have established credibility and earned people's trust by repeatedly assisting disadvantaged communities in the face of poverty, natural disasters, and conflicts. Companies are beginning to work with such organizations to break into new markets. For instance, Telenor has teamed up with Grameen Bank to sell cellular telephones to rural consumers. Telenor has taken advantage of the bank's knowledge of rural microcredit groups' collection and payment system to set up a joint venture, Grameen Phone, in which it has a 62% equity stake. Similarly, World Diagnostics found that, in Uganda, it could best sell its HIV, STD, and malaria test kits through NGO-operated health care networks. The NGOs are helping villagers deal with AIDS, and they have trained medical personnel, set up clinics, and earned the trust of Ugandans along the way.

At the same time, declines worldwide in public spending on social programs have forced NGOs to review their traditional poverty reduction strategies. Where NGOs once saw government aid and private sector charity as the only ways out of poverty, they now see entrepreneurship, too, as a viable approach. They've reframed the poor as "undercapitalized, unappreciated, and undersupported entrepreneurs," and redefined poverty as a problem of "livelihoods development." NGOs such as Care developed this livelihood-oriented approach, providing poor people with training, credit, and collective business infrastructure. Consequently, social groups have discovered business opportunities among their constituents, and scores of social venture capital funds have emerged to support this strategy.

Thus, while companies have discovered the importance of NGOs as paths to markets, social groups have realized that carefully calibrated business models can unleash powerful forces for good. Their interactions have created new links between business innovation and social development. As we shall see in the following pages, companies and NGOs are increasingly going into business together, pursuing scale and profits, social equity, and empowerment as part of an integrated value chain.

The Path to Convergence

Sometimes the best way to understand the future is to look back. When we do, we can see that the relationship between companies and NGOs is moving beyond an adversarial stance toward partnership through systematic, if uncharted, steps. This journey has so far progressed through three phases, each of which has had its teething problems, naysayers, tensions, and benefits. (See "The Three Stages in the Convergence Between the Corporate Sector and the Civil Society" at the end of this article.)

THE BE-RESPONSIBLE STAGE

By the late 1980s, companies and NGOs realized that they couldn't keep fighting; they had to find ways of living with and influencing each other. Some felt they could take the risk of working with the other side to meet specific, albeit limited, objectives. That was the most difficult step; executives and activists had to reexamine perceptions and biases. They had to evaluate the risks to their identities, to their missions, and to their industry standing before they could collaborate with "the enemy."

"Corporate social responsibility" has become a catchall phrase for the ways by which businesses manage reputations and strike relationships with the social sector. Businesses use their resources to work on socially relevant issues as they are defined by NGOs, but most CSR initiatives, such as Exxon Mobil's involvement in the distribution of mosquito nets in Tanzania or General Motors' management of children's education programs in the United States, are unrelated to the companies' core business activities. Some NGOs are willing to work with companies to establish policy dialogues and social programs, but they keep their corporate supporters at arm's length. The pros and cons of CSR have been explored elsewhere (see, for instance, Allen L. White's 2005 report, "Fade, Integrate or Transform: The Future of CSR"), but what is relevant to our story are three convergences that it created:

The convergence of standards of practice and the emergence of joint regulatory frameworks. As companies built relationships with NGOs, the two sides adopted joint regulatory schemes. The civil society and the corporate sector together manage, for instance, the Apparel Industry Partnership, the Forest Stewardship Council, the Marine Stewardship Council, and the Kimberley Process (in the diamond business), which stipulate social and environmental practices in their respective industries. Through these mechanisms, companies have gained access to NGOs' knowledge about local markets and social networks, while social groups have developed more expertise in marketing and specialized business practices.

The convergence of brands, marketing, and communications, and the emergence of the first joint platforms for marketing and customer management. Cause-related marketing captures this trend best. That's when a company markets its products or services to an NGO's loyalists, and the NGO markets itself to the company's customers and employees, generating revenues for both the company and the NGO's charitable activities. In 2005, cause-related marketing initiatives provided around $1 billion to social causes in North America alone. The approach has enabled the two sectors to learn each other's marketing tactics. Now, for instance, some companies use viral-marketing techniques, which NGOs pioneered, while several social groups commission professional advertising firms to design advocacy campaigns. Through such joint-marketing relationships, companies and NGOs have shifted from constructing divergent messages for polarized audiences to creating similar messages for a common audience.

The convergence of professional cadres and career paths, and the emergence of management professionals dedicated to working with companies on social causes and with NGOs on business endeavors. Today, the human rights manager (at Monsanto), the senior manager for corporate responsibility (at Nike), and the sustainable development manager (at Marks and Spencer) work with counterparts at NGOs like the vice president for private sector partnerships at Conservation International. Once, activists would have labeled NGO professionals as sellouts if they went to work with companies, but NGO veterans now hold the communications, community relations, and market development portfolios at several companies. Executives who previously would have signaled their early retirement if they took positions at NGOs find themselves among a cohort of social venture capitalists. In fact, many managers are building their careers by moving back and forth between the two sectors. (We describe the implications of these areas of convergence for the next phase of partnership in the exhibit "How Companies and NGOs Find Common Ground.")

Broadly speaking, CSR started as a way for companies to gather intelligence about NGOs and manage their reputations, and it has wound up providing them with the tools they need to pursue business opportunities in untapped markets. For NGOs, CSR began as a means of persuading companies to change their ways, and it has become a means for them to develop the competencies and confidence to go into business themselves. CSR therefore laid some of the foundations on which corporations and social groups each started experimenting with new business models.

THE GET-INTO-BUSINESS STAGE

After more than 15 years of globalization, transnational companies have made headway in only the most affluent segments of the developing world. As a percentage of GDP, for example, flows of foreign direct investment to developing countries in Asia and Latin America were no greater in fiscal 2004 than they were in fiscal 1995. These miniscule inflows signal the failure of multinational corporations to change their business models to serve the largest consumer segment in the world: the 4 billion to 5 billion consumers at the bottom of the pyramid. Barring a few exceptions in the telecommunications and fast-moving consumer goods industries, Western companies have performed poorly in serving these customers. For instance, multinational water companies, even in supportive environments like South Africa, have all but given up trying to manage urban water systems. The food-retailing industry operates approximately one store for every 3.4 million people in low-income countries compared with one store per 5,800 people in high-income countries, according to CIES, a food industry trade association based in Paris. Foreign insurance giants have failed to create customer bases in low-income markets. The list of failures and near failures is long.

When companies have succeeded in bottom-of-the-pyramid markets, we found, they have most often done it by leveraging the competencies, networks, and business models that were developed as part of their CSR initiatives or by NGOs. ABN AMRO has entered the microfinance business in Latin America with some help from the NGO Accion International. Barclays has built a successful microbanking operation in Ghana in partnership with 4,000 indigenous moneylenders and their national association. The Shell Foundation has worked with environmental NGOs to test new designs and models for delivering clean and renewable energy to underserved populations. It has created venture capital funds that support local entrepreneurs and integrate them into Royal Dutch Shell's supply chains.

Pick 'n Pay, one of South Africa's largest retailers, started a CSR initiative in the early 1990s to support

How Companies and NGOs Find Common Ground

CHALLENGES AND INNOVATIONS

CONVERGENCE AREA	EXAMPLES	Corporate	NGO
Pooling knowledge, competencies, and relationships to build new operating standards and coregulatory schemes.	• The Apparel Industry Partnership • The Forest Stewardship Council • The Marine Stewardship Council • The Kimberley Process	**The Challenge** To move from adhering to individual company standards to compliance with industrywide standards. **Innovative Responses** Companies are • Defining standards through negotiations with NGOs. • Building the ability to participate in global and local NGO networks, forums, boards, and so forth.	**The Challenge** To move from spearheading anti-business campaigns to creating, promoting, and jointly administering standards. **Innovative Responses** NGOs are • Defining standards through negotiation with companies. • Learning to understand microlevel industry operations in, for example, forestry, fishing, and mining.
Leveraging each other's credibility and social networks to create access to markets and brand value.	• Companies have set up cause-related marketing as a new area of specialization. • In 2005, companies spent $1 billion in North America on cause-related marketing.	**The Challenge** To redefine NGOs as consumer clusters that require special messages and management. **Innovative Responses** Companies are • Adopting NGOs' marketing approaches, such as viral marketing.	**The Challenge** To professionalize brand management. **Innovative Responses** NGOs are • Cobranding campaigns with companies.

Creating professional development norms and management roles to facilitate coordination between the two sectors.	• Delivering on special brand promises. • Shifting from a reactive to a proactive approach to social sector communications.	• Marketing themselves to corporate partners' customers and employees, instead of making appeals to the public. • Facing stricter fiscal controls to separate economic decisions from policy decisions.
The Challenge		
	To integrate CSR into business decision making.	To cooperate with companies in some forums and disagree in others.
Innovative Responses		
• Rather than two distinct camps and career paths, companies and NGOs recruit staff from each other. • The two sectors use a common service industry—the same marketing or law firm, for instance. • A plethora of bisector training forums, including social sector MBA programs, are born.	Companies are • Aligning strategies for building material assets and reputations. • Integrating social and financial reporting. • Managing cooperation with NGOs in cause-related marketing and public-policy forums. • Encouraging managers to sit on NGO boards and granting leaves of absence to managers doing social sector work.	NGOs are • Creating organizations that seek common ground on policy issues, and facilitate partnerships, with companies. • Integrating activist and business management mentalities into the organization. • Establishing new professional norms related to nondisclosure of sensitive corporate information.

struggling black farmers and their weak cooperatives, who were left on the edge of financial viability by apartheid. The foundation helped strengthen the cooperatives by providing them with management and marketing skills. When apartheid ended in 1994, Pick 'n Pay immediately started exploring how it could serve people in urban townships. The retailer found that there was an opportunity in providing those consumers with produce that came from their rural homelands. To meet that demand, Pick 'n Pay used the relationships its foundation had struck to develop reliable suppliers of traditional produce. Later, Pick 'n Pay used the same approach to create another supply chain for organic produce. (For more examples, see C. K. Prahalad's *The Fortune at the Bottom of the Pyramid: Eradicating Poverty Through Profits.*)

At the same time, social groups have also set up businesses, usually entering market segments where corporations had been unsuccessful. In 1992, the amount NGOs gave out in development assistance was equal to about 11% of the funds governments in developed countries donated; by 2003, that amount had risen to 16%. In that year, grants from NGOs represented a remarkable 9.4% of public and private development assistance from OECD countries and multilateral agencies, according to the OECD's "Development Co-operation Report 2005." NGOs have used their funds to develop the infrastructure needed to supply people in remote areas with food, medicine, other supplies, and credit when disasters strike. Along the way, they acquired firsthand knowledge of underserved markets and gained credibility with local communities.

For instance, after the 2004 tsunami, NGOs in India built microcredit operations as part of the relief effort. In

Africa, international NGOs such as Africare and Direct Relief International, together with local groups, built infrastructure to deal with AIDS, famines, and refugee influxes. Along with microcredit and mutual insurance operations, they developed informal networks of traders and state-owned organizations into cooperatives, federations, and export-oriented enterprises. In India, NGOs like the Self Employed Women's Association (SEWA) are working with Indian insurance companies (such as ICICI Prudential), savings and credit cooperatives, and mutual health associations to sell insurance products. In Africa, supported by Western NGOs like Care and Finca International, local NGOs such as L'Association pour le Développement de la Région de Kaya (ADRK) in Burkina Faso, the Malawi Union of Savings and Credit Cooperatives, MicroSave (in Kenya), and Faitière des Unités Coopératives d'Epargne et de Crédit du Togo are selling crop, rain, life, asset-loss, widowhood, health, personal accident, and maternity insurance products to low-income consumers. In Uganda, Microcare has completed a three-year pilot that caters to 3,000 people. The project is being commercialized by a new for-profit company, Microcare Health, which has been set up jointly by Microcare and the Chicago-based insurer Aon.

Some NGOs are positively thriving where state-owned or multinational companies have failed. Two years ago, when the Indian insurance giant, Life Insurance Corporation, found it difficult to collect premiums and pay claims in rural areas in the state of Andhra Pradesh, microcredit federations took over the business. Their extensive knowledge of customers and their superior reach allowed the NGOs to grow the market rapidly. They operate quite profitably, earning an average gross margin of 27%.

As the scale and sophistication of their businesses grow, NGOs have become powerful national players. For instance, in 1986, a small group of street traders formed the African Co-operative for Hawkers and Informal Businesses to fight for their rights. ACHIB today counts 120,000 members in South Africa. It advocates hawkers' interests on policy matters and provides them with support services, such as warehousing infrastructure, bulk procurement, product distribution, microloans, and training. Recently, ACHIB launched a soft drink brand called Hola, which it distributes through a for-profit entity, Main Market Distribution. The cooperative has also entered the advertising business by launching hawker stalls with spaces that big companies can rent, in its words, "to increase awareness for their brands in the informal market."

The Minneapolis-based HealthStore Foundation represents a new breed of nonprofit that is designed from its inception to operate as a business. The foundation was set up by a small group of business professionals who had worked with NGOs in Africa to provide people with safe medicines. It used a franchise model to create 68 owner-operated Child & Family Wellness Shops, which sell health services and medicine in small towns in three districts in Kenya. The outlets operate according to common performance standards, and the HealthStore Foundation provides them with turnkey management systems and support, training owners and helping them select locations that will allow them to serve at least 5,000 households. In 2005, the clinics treated 404,000 patients; buoyed by their success, the NGO plans to set up 30 more outlets in 2007. In addition to private donations, foundation grants, and social venture capital funds, HealthStore also accepts grants from companies.

Some NGOs, like Accion, have succeeded in building multinational businesses. Acting as an agent for large microfinance NGOs, Accion has loaned $9.4 billion to 4 million people in 22 countries, with a historical repayment rate greater than 97%. In 1992, Accion helped create the first bank in the world dedicated solely to microenterprise—BancoSol in Bolivia. Several of Accion's partners have made the transition from being charity-dependent organizations to becoming banks or other regulated financial institutions. Accion has also helped commercial banks—such as Sogebank in Haiti, Banco del Pichincha in Ecuador, and Banco ABN AMRO Real in Brazil—lend to the self-employed poor. In the United States, Accion has worked with Bank of America and Wachovia to identify potential clients who do not meet standard lending requirements.

The growing strength of NGO-owned businesses in emerging markets is mirrored in developed countries. Nonprofits have been pioneers in trading carbon emissions, producing organic foods, manufacturing herbal supplements, providing pay-as-you-go car-rental services, and many other businesses. For example, Local Sustainability is an Ontario-based NGO that provides engineering and energy management–consulting services to municipalities. It has succeeded where the likes of GE Capital, Philips Utilities, and Ameresco have struggled, owing to the high costs involved in getting political, bureaucratic, and technical representatives of municipalities to invest in making facilities more energy efficient. Through its expertise in generating political commitment for energy and environmental measures, Local Sustainability has been able to land 36 municipalities in Canada and the United States as customers. In the process, it has generated $2.5 million in revenues and earned a 50% gross margin. Rivals initially criticized the NGO, claiming its not-for-profit status was a public subsidy, but consulting firms such as CH2M Hill now work closely with Local Sustainability because of its skills and reputation.

Before we describe the third stage of company-NGO relations, we must point out that the drive to set up businesses has created tensions within the two sectors. First, both companies and social groups are finding it difficult to manage their new roles. What does a multinational corporation such as Royal Dutch Shell do with the Shell Foundation when it shifts to a "business investment strategy in order to achieve both social and investment goals?" Will an NGO like Local Sustainability better achieve its objective of making facilities more energy efficient by spinning off its consultancy as a for-profit operation or by managing it as a project within its nonprofit structure? The answers aren't clear.

Second, NGOs are often unsure whether a company is a potential collaborator or competitor, and vice versa. On the one hand, nonprofit ventures such as Local Sustainability in Canada and microinsurance networks in India are bagging customers that corporations would dearly love to have. On the other hand, health food retailers such as Whole Foods Market have taken away customers who used to shop at NGO-owned cooperatives. Retailers like Starbucks and Tesco sell products that compete with the NGOs' Fairtrade line of products. Since the companies buy fewer Fairtrade products as result, the turn of events is worrying to the NGOs that created the standard.

Reactions to competition at the bottom of the pyramid can be complicated. ICICI became the biggest manager of microcredit operations in the south Indian state of Tamil Nadu by co-opting the women's microcredit groups that NGOs developed. Many NGOs are resigned to this; ICICI offers a larger range of banking services and provides greater opportunities for entrepreneurs. However, other groups are unhappy that ICICI has taken over their role and the women's self-help groups that they had designed for broader social development purposes. Some are reluctant to forge business relationships with the bank as a result.

THE COCREATE-BUSINESSES STAGE

As more companies conduct business experiments in bottom-of-the-pyramid markets and NGOs' business acumen evolves, they are realizing each other's limitations and strengths. This has laid the foundation for long-term partnerships between the two sectors based on "cocreation." Cocreation involves the development of an integrated business model in which the company becomes a key part of the NGO's capacity to deliver value and vice versa. Such ventures offer three opportunities:

- To deliver products at low prices to low-income consumers or to provide niche products to consumers in mature markets.

- To create hybrid business models involving corporations, NGOs, and entrepreneurs at the bottom of the economic ladder.

- To revive the corporation's social legitimacy while expanding the NGO's impact.

When companies and NGOs innovate together, the commercial nature of the relationship and their roles can vary, but the outcome is often a breakthrough. In fact, this quiet dialogue, away from public debates, has spawned key principles that will underlie governance structures in the future, as "The New Rules of Company-NGO Engagement," at the end of this article, shows. Take the case of BP (formerly British Petroleum), which set out to develop a fuel-efficient stove for poor consumers in rural India. Market research showed that consumers wanted the option of switching fuels based on their current income, the availability of fuels, and cooking styles. Working with the Indian Institute of Science in Bangalore, BP developed a portable stove that could use either liquefied petroleum gas (LPG) or biomass as fuel. To meet an additional social objective, BP designed the stove to burn biomass very efficiently, which would eliminate the smoke that causes respiratory illnesses in India.

One of BP's major challenges is distribution and retailing, since only small shops and informal traders cater to villagers in rural India. The company found that if it were to invest in building the distribution infrastructure from scratch, it wouldn't be able to sell the stove at a price that its target customers could afford. BP realized that it would have to work with local people who knew rural consumers and had access to distribution agents in the villages. Although the company could hire marketing experts or social workers as consultants, it wanted to develop relationships cheaply with scores of agents so that it could serve a linguistically disparate, culturally diverse, and physically dispersed customer base. While conducting preliminary market research, BP's managers met with three NGOs—Covenant Centre of Development, IDPMS, and Swayam Shikshan Prayog—that operated microcredit operations and other social enterprises in south India.

BP and the NGOs conducted market research together in order to become acquainted with each other's motivations, standards, and capabilities. After that, the two sides defined a shared strategic intent and developed a set of working principles. They built trust through relationships established between key individuals. Trust grew when BP made a long-term contractual commitment to the project. That trust proved to be pivotal, for instance, when the NGOs decided to consolidate distribution channels in five states to generate economies of scale. Most companies prefer to work with several distributors to spread their risks, but BP, understanding the NGOs' pressures, backed the consolidation. The NGOs established a new company that serves as a joint business vehicle through which village agents can pool their investments, licenses, and risk. That was new; the social groups had never before set up a joint operation with one another or with a corporation.

The two sides worked with each other closely at every stage of the project. They refined the business model, developed the rollout plans, and executed them through joint working groups. BP and the NGOs worked together to identify markets and train the distribution agents. They jointly evaluated the stove's design, costs, usability, and safety. They held discussions about the economics of production, distribution, consumer offers (including financing), capital investment, returns, and risks for everyone involved—not only BP and the NGOs but also customers, distributors, and microcredit federations.

BP and the NGOs also tackled the nonnegotiable issues in tandem. BP, for instance, would not compromise on safety standards for the transportation, storage, and use of LPG or violate its own standards of business ethics. Health and safety standards became a central part of the NGO training curriculum; the NGOs' employees even had to learn to use seat belts while driving around. For their part, the NGOs wanted to protect their credibility and goodwill with villagers. BP therefore had to make some accommodations, as well. The company had to ensure, for instance, that the women the NGO's company recruited as local sales agents were the first to receive cash generated by the business, thus allowing the villagers to recover their working capital.

The manner in which BP and the NGOs struck a commercial agreement bears no resemblance to traditional supplier-channel deals. One difference is the transparency about cost structures and margins. The NGOs, for instance, conducted an analysis of the distribution process, identifying every cost element and breakeven scenario related to LPG cylinders, which are heavier, more regulated, and more dangerous than the products the NGOs usually handle. They conveyed the findings to BP. Suppliers often withhold information from distributors to gain an upper hand during negotiations. In this instance, BP and the NGOs shared their internal economics with each other so they could understand all the choices they faced in terms of distribution costs, consumer service options, growth rates, and breakeven points. This unusual level of transparency helped overcome the traditional mistrust between the two sectors.

Finally, BP and the NGOs developed a financial model that would allow everyone in the value chain to make money. The NGOs had to assume a great deal of the credit risks and legal liabilities for the agents in the villages. They would not have done so unless they were confident that BP was making a long-term investment in the project. The multinational had to reveal business data it would not normally share with distributors. Drawing up the legal contracts that captured the cocreation-based relationship was a huge learning and confidence-building experience, according to managers on both sides. The process engendered a culture of frankness, transparency, and joint problem solving that is unique in the history of company-NGO relationships.

The benefits of the cocreation approach will have to stand the test of the market, but some advantages are already evident. First, involving credible NGOs that have extensive infrastructure on the ground was tremendously valuable to BP, a foreign company with limited experience in India and no experience with any rural bottom-of-the-pyramid market. Second, the NGOs participated in a complex product-design process and in developing a business model. Doing so benefited them in two ways: They shared in the credit for developing the stove, and they gained credibility as successful collaborators with a global firm. Third, both the company and the NGOs have brought unique balance-sheet advantages to a new business. BP's deep pockets and patience can withstand the trials of a start-up; the NGOs can quickly access other assets, such as land, that the business needs. Finally, BP and the NGOs have together developed a business ecosystem that brings different economic entities—a global corporation, local social organizations, informal micro-entrepreneurs, and a research institute—into an efficient value chain. This alliance offers the promise of more than just access to better products at more affordable prices; it gives people at the bottom of the pyramid, who until now were unable to enjoy the benefits of globalization, a chance to create new livelihoods and gain economic and social influence.

T HE SAME PATTERN is visible in the cocreation partnerships between ABN AMRO and Accion; Telenor, Danone, and Grameen Bank; Microsoft and Pratham;

ICICI Prudential and SEWA; Local Sustainability and CH2M Hill; Microcare and Aon. In all these cases, neither company nor NGO can see the other as an adversary because of their interdependence; both apply assets and competencies to a business that creates greater value for each than their independent efforts could generate. We can judge these partnerships' performance by the level of value they deliver to customers and communities: Companies and NGOs now both share the pressure to perform, cutting through the spin that has too long dominated our understanding of globalization and its opportunities.

The Three Stages in the Convergence Between the Corporate Sector and the Civil Society

Preconvergence

Companies and NGOs adopt different attitudes toward liberalization and globalization. They quarrel over the nature and speed of deregulation. They fight over companies' conduct, especially in developing countries.

Stage One

Companies and NGOs realize they have to coexist. They look for ways to influence each other. Some corporations and NGOs execute joint social responsibility projects.

Stage Two

Some companies get into bottom-of-the-pyramid segments and niche markets even as NGOs set up businesses in those markets. Companies and NGOs try to learn from, and work with, each other.

Stage Three

Companies and NGOs enter into cocreation business relationships. Cocreation entails the development of business models in which companies become a key part of NGOs' capacity to deliver value and vice versa.

The New Rules of Company-NGO Engagement

AS COMPANIES AND NGOS work together, they are jointly defining the norms that will govern their future relations and behavior.

- The private and civil society sectors will cocreate markets, along with emerging customers and bottom-of-the-pyramid entrepreneurs, through innovative business models.

- Task-oriented relationships, rather than ideology or policy-driven dialogues, will emerge as the mode of collaboration between companies and NGOs.

- NGOs and companies will need to align global positions and standards and be very local in their ability to serve customers and create value.

- Since both external governance processes and the level of developmental benefits will be internal to the new business models, neither companies nor NGOs can see one another as adversaries.

- Companies and NGOs will gain legitimacy in society by creating bold value propositions that have credible economic, social, and environmental dimensions.

- Companies and NGOs will be under pressure to advocate common policy positions and jointly develop coregulatory schemes.

Originally published in February 2007
Reprint R0702D

About the Contributors

IAN BREMMER is the president of Eurasia Group, a political-risk consulting firm, and a senior fellow at the World Policy Institute in New York.

JEB BRUGMANN is a Toronto-based consultant who works for companies to develop business models for the underserved segments of emerging markets.

RICHARD BURKHOLDER is the Director of International Polling at Gallup Poll. He is also the Regional Research Director for the Middle East, North Africa, and other predominantly Muslim countries throughout the world for the Gallup World Poll.

GURCHARAN DAS is the former chairman and managing director of Procter & Gamble India. Currently he is an author, consultant, and public intellectual.

XIAOGUANG FANG is the vice chairman of Gallup China.

ORIT GADIESH is the chairman of Bain & Company in Boston.

ALLEN HAMMOND is VP for Innovation and Special Projects at the World Resources Institute. He also directs WRI's Development Through Enterprise project.

TARUN KHANNA is the Jorge Paulo Lehmann Professor at Harvard Business School.

PHILIP LEUNG is a Bain partner in Shanghai and leads the firm's Greater China health care practice.

WILLIAM MCEWEN is a global practice leader in brand management for the Gallup Organization.

C. K. PRAHALAD is the Paul and Ruth McCracken Distinguished University Professor of Corporate Strategy at the University of Michigan's Ross School of Business in Ann Arbor.

KRISHNA G. PALEPU is the Ross Graham Walker Professor of Business Administration and Senior Associate Dean for International Development at Harvard Business School.

JAYANT SINHA is a partner at McKinsey & Company in New Delhi.

TILL VESTRING, a Bain & Company partner based in Singapore, leads the firm's Asia Pacific industrial practice.

CHUANPING ZHANG is a managing partner at Gallup Poll.

Index